Training Your Mixed Breed

A KENNEL CLUB BOOK®

AUTHOR BIOGRAPHY

The author, Miriam Fields-Babineau, with Golden Retriever puppies.

Miriam Fields-Babineau has been training dogs and other animals professionally since 1978. She has owned and operated Training Unlimited Animal Training and Animal Actors, Inc., for 25 years. She teaches people how to communicate with and train their dogs, of any age or breed, specializing in behavioral problem-solving.

Ms. Fields-Babineau has authored many animal-related books, including *Dog Training with a Head Halter* (Barron's Educational Series, Inc.), the e-book *How to Become a Professional Dog Trainer* (Intellectua.com), *Dog Training Basics* (Sterling Publishing Co., Inc.) and many more. She writes numerous articles for trade magazines, such as the award-winning *Off-Lead Magazine* and *Practical Horseman*. She has produced the videos *The First Hello*, which addresses how to prepare a dog for an infant, and *Dog Training with a Comfort Trainer*, which demonstrates how to train a dog using her head-halter design, the Comfort Trainer.

Ms. Fields-Babineau also provides animals for television, film and advertising, having worked with *National Geographic*, Animal Planet, the History Channel, Warner Films, Orion Films, the Discovery Channel, CBS, the Family Channel and many more. When not training other people's animal companions, she travels the country, performing in equine and canine competitions as well as exhibiting the skills of her trained felines.

Photographs by:
Mary Bloom, Bernd Brinkmann, Evan Cohen, Billy Deputato, Christopher Deputato, Tracey & Erik Erath, Miriam Fields-Babineau, Isabelle Français, Amy Gilbert, Mary Ieronimo, Carol Ann Johnson, Jose Martinez, Tammy & Rich Phelan, Dennis Spring, Penni Stagg, Donyale Testa and Alice van Kempen.

The publisher would like to thank all of the owners of the dogs featured in this book.

KENNEL CLUB BOOKS: TRAINING YOUR MIXED BREED
ISBN: 1-59378-592-5

Copyright © 2005 Kennel Club Books, LLC
308 Main Street, Allenhurst, NJ 07711 USA
Cover Design Patented: US 6,435,559 B2 • Printed in South Korea

10 9 8 7 6 5 4 3 2 1

Training Your Mixed Breed

By Miriam Fields-Babineau

CONTENTS

The Making of the Mixed Breed

Learn the background of the mixed-breed dog and what traits a mix may have based on his lineage. Explore the general characteristics of the major breed groups and, more specifically, of popular breeds that are commonly seen in mixes to help you learn about what traits your mixed-breed dog might have or to help you determine his ancestry if unknown.

Selecting Your Dog

Discuss the process of finding a mixed-breed puppy or dog through an animal shelter, humane society or rescue organization. Learn how to interpret a dog's body language to learn about his personality. Formal temperament testing exercises, scoring and interpretation are also presented, as well as the importance of socializing your new dog.

Caring for Your Dog

Acquaint yourself with the basics of how to keep your dog happy and healthy. Topics discussed include proper feeding, home safety, grooming, veterinary care, home health-care checks, special needs of certain body types and how to keep your dog constructively occupied to promote good behavior.

Basic Training and Good Manners

Follow a plan for house-training success. Learn about common bad habits in dogs and how to prevent and cure them. Train your dog the positive way, using targeting and positive-reinforcement techniques to teach the basic commands and correct undesirable behaviors. Also discussed are working with a professional trainer and the proper use of a head halter.

Fun and Games

Training isn't all work and no play! Discover the various competitive sports available to you and your dog through the clubs and organizations that include mixed breeds. Learn some fun tricks to teach your dog, including "shake," "wave," "roll over" and more, and introduce some games like retrieving and differentiating between toys.

An adorable
young terrier mix,
Willi, is enjoying
a sunny day.

THE MAKING OF THE MIXED BREED

IN THE MIX

According to the Mixed Breed Dog Clubs of America, a mixed-breed dog is the offspring of two pure-bred dogs of different breeds. The pairing of a pure-bred with a mixed breed produces mongrels and, if both sire and dam are mixed breeds, then the offspring are mutts. Regardless of definition, a dog that is not identifiable as a pure-bred is not allowed to compete in events offered solely for pure-breds by the American Kennel Club (AKC) and specialty clubs. However, there are several national and international clubs devoted to furthering the sport of mixed-breed dogs. These include

Mario is a Chihuahua mix whose small size belies his huge personality.

the aforementioned Mixed Breed Dog Clubs of America, North American Mixed Breed Registry and various local and regional mixed-breed dog clubs. Several pure-bred dog clubs do allow mixed breeds to compete at their events. These clubs include the United Kennel Club, North American Dog Racing Association and Australian Shepherd Club of America. All of these organizations recognize that mixed-breed dogs are able to train and compete on the same levels as pure-bred dogs.

One cannot state that a mixed-breed dog is any more or less healthy, intelligent or long-lived than a pure-bred. These factors depend more on the dog's genetics and lifetime care. However, it has been noted that mixed-breed dogs are less likely to contract some of

Bella is a Beagle/Coonhound mix, pictured here in her new home just a few weeks after being adopted from a shelter.

the common hereditary problems that can be seen in pure-breds. These problems occur sometimes as a result of poor breeding and sometimes because certain conditions are difficult to detect no matter how careful the breeder. Common hereditary disorders include hip and elbow dysplasia, retinal atrophy and heart defects, among others. A mixed-breed dog may draw strength from the background of one of his ancestors to overcome the weaknesses of another. He also may gain certain propensities from both sides of his lineage. He may be able to show the abilities to both herd sheep and find lost people, instead of the specialized abilities of the herding dog who is bred solely for herding or the working dog developed solely for search-and-rescue.

All dog breeds were developed for specific tasks. There are breeds that guard, breeds that herd, breeds that have specialized hunting skills and breeds that were meant to warm the hands and feet of their human companions. Your mixed-breed dog is a combination of one or more of these, making him unique unto himself, a pawprint of individuality. Unlike with a pure-bred dog, you will not be able to foretell his exact size or personal-

This dog, an interesting mix of Airedale Terrier, Doberman Pinscher and Schnauzer, grew up to resemble a wiry-coated Doberman.

ity until he is fully developed. You will be able to tell certain things, like whether he has long fur or a short coat, floppy ears or erect ones. He may end up weighing 25, 55 or over 100 pounds! Knowledge of who his parents are and how big he is as a pup will give you an idea of eventual size, but there is still no guarantee. Most owners of mixed breeds have no idea of parentage, so the best means of knowing is by learning about the attributes of pure-breds and applying them to observed behaviors and appearances in their mixed-breed dogs. Their genetic codes contain similar information. Size, conformation, coat coloration and even some similarities in behavior can be noted. However, this can often be difficult to decipher while your mixed-breed dog is young.

Knowing more about pure-bred dogs will aid you in better understanding your own mixed breed. Will the dog be suitable in a home with a family that works long hours? How will he get along with young children? Will the dog have a tendency to be hyperactive? Even though the behavioral tendencies of a pure breed can be more predictable, there are individuals that often vary from the norm.

If you know something about your lovely individual, such as the breed(s) of one or both parents, you will have some idea as to what to expect throughout his development, leading to a better under-

Perhaps the most universally loved dog in the world, the Labrador Retriever.

standing of his overall behavior patterns and physical attributes. If you do not have breed specifics, then you hopefully will at least be able to determine to which group of dogs one or both parents belonged, such as the terriers, sporting dogs, hounds and so on. For explanation purposes, we will discuss the breed groups according to AKC classification.

EXPLORING THE BREED GROUPS

SPORTING GROUP
Two of America's most popular breeds belong to the Sporting Group: the Labrador Retriever and the Golden Retriever. Other popular breeds in this group are the Cocker Spaniel, German Shorthaired Pointer, English Springer Spaniel, Weimaraner, Vizsla, Brittany and Chesapeake

The Golden Retriever is not far behind the Lab in popularity, known for his beauty, zest for life and gregarious personality.

Bay Retriever. Among the less common breeds seen in the group are handsome pointing breeds like the German Wirehaired Pointer and Wirehaired Pointing Griffon; terrific retrievers including the Curly-Coated Retriever, Flat-Coated Retriever and Nova Scotia Duck Tolling Retriever; some elegant setting dogs like the English Setter and Gordon Setter; and, of course, those wonderful spaniels—the Clumber Spaniel, English Cocker Spaniel, American Water Spaniel, Field Spaniel, Irish Water Spaniel, Sussex Spaniel and Welsh Springer Spaniel. Any of these breeds would be less likely to be involved in a "mixed

The Chesapeake Bay Retriever is a top-notch field dog with a more aloof personality than the other retriever breeds.

marriage" than the more popular and more numerous breeds.

Sporting dogs were originally bred to aid hunters. From flushing and fetching to pointing and chasing, sporting dogs are bred for specific hunting conditions and types of game. These breeds have lots of energy, are very loyal and are eager to please. They love people and activities. Most sporting dogs make great family pets because of their trainability and love of family social events. They do not do well in homes with children under five years of age, for they are very active and may inadvertently knock small children over, but they can keep up with older children and stay active well into their senior years.

Sporting breeds are usually very friendly and eager to be part of the family unit. They do not do well if cooped up in small areas for long periods of time or left alone without a chance to play with people and other dogs. They require lots of exercise and do not care about the weather conditions as much as some other breeds. Most, in fact, have been bred to retrieve from the water, so they don't understand why they cannot go out to play on a rainy day. Should your mixed-breed dog contain sporting-dog traits, be sure to pay attention to these traits and how strongly they are expressed. For example, a dog that is half Labrador Retriever and half

Dalmatian (classified as Non-Sporting but an extremely active breed derived from pointing dogs) may be all black but have the long legs of the Dalmatian. This will be a high-energy dog. He also may be very demanding of your attention.

Since Golden Retrievers and Labrador Retrievers are among the most popular breeds of dog, there are many mixed-breed dogs whose lineage has some percentage of one or both of these breeds. Luckily, Labs and Goldens have many desirable qualities. They are easy to train and care for, and they are great with people of all ages. Goldens tend to be a little more sensitive than Labradors, and therefore should never be dealt with harshly. Labrador Retrievers require owners who are persistent and patient, but not overly harsh. Goldens stand up to 24 inches at the shoulders and can weigh up to 75 pounds, while Labs can be a little taller and somewhat heavier. Goldens have medium-length coats with feathering on their legs, tails and necks. Their coats range from buff to dark gold or red, whereas Labradors are seen in black, chocolate and yellow and have short coats. Regardless of their coat lengths, both breeds shed significantly.

In the last few years, people have been crossing Standard Poodles with Labrador Retrievers and Golden Retrievers. The result is a fabulous mixed-breed dog called the Labradoodle and

Lab/German Shepherd mix Daisy and Pit Bull mix Misty are frequent playmates and two of the sweetest dogs around.

Goldendoodle that is intelligent, sensitive and affectionate, very much like the original retriever, the Curly-Coated Retriever.

After the Lab and Golden, the Chesapeake Bay Retriever is the next-highest retriever in AKC registration numbers. Chessies are rugged and powerful. Their curly coats are waterproof and range in color from sandy to deep brown. They can weigh up to 80 pounds and stand up to 26 inches at the shoulders. Chessies also have the classic retriever attribute of webbed feet. These dogs are great hunting partners but do not

The Brittany is a friendly, active, naturally appealing spaniel.

The German Shorthaired Pointer is a skilled hunting companion, striking in his liver coat, which often has white markings.

normally fit in as well in urban or suburban environments. They can be very protective and sometimes aggressive with other dogs. This is not the best breed for a family with young children.

Overall, pointing breeds are long-legged and lean of torso. Most have pendant ears. They tend to stand "frozen" in position with their tails straight out and a forepaw lifted when confronted with game or something new. One

such pointer, the Brittany, friendly and happy, has a medium-length, slightly wavy coat that varies from orange to liver on white. The breed can reach up to 20.5 inches at the shoulder and can weigh up to 40 pounds. Brittanys adore interaction with family members and thrive on direction.

German Shorthaired Pointers are very energetic dogs that prefer being out in the field to being cooped up indoors. They do not do well in urban or suburban environments. They need room to run and roam or will otherwise become difficult to handle. They can be stubborn at times and reserved but, if socialized early, will fit into families with older children and active lifestyles. They stand up to 25 inches at the shoulder and can reach 70 pounds. Their short coats can be solid liver or liver with white patches and freckles.

The German Wirehaired Pointer is not as numerous as his shorthaired cousin, but is equally as talented and handsome, with trademark facial furnishings.

Setter breeds have long silky ears that hang down beyond their chins. English Setters are mostly white with orange, lemon, liver or black markings, the latter sometimes with tan points. They are high-energy dogs that require persistent training and lots of exercise. They stand up to 25 inches at the shoulder and can weigh up to 70 pounds. There is a difference in type seen between show and field English Setters. The field dogs are smaller and lighter, with shorter coats. The English Setter is fairly often seen mixed with other breeds.

Irish Setters are high-energy dogs that stand about 25 to 27 inches at the shoulder and can weigh up to 70 pounds. They have medium-length coats with feathering at their legs, tails and chests. Their coats are silky, in shades of red from light chestnut to dark mahogany. These dogs do well with people and other dogs but require consistent direction or they can easily pick up on bad habits. This is another popular breed, but rarely found mixed with other breeds due to careful breeding practices.

Spaniel breeds come in all shapes and sizes. The ever-popular Cocker Spaniel is often purposely bred with the Poodle to produce the Cockapoo, a pleasant mix known to be cute, cuddly and intelligent. Cocker Spaniels have been quite popular among dog

owners since the 1960s and their favor continues today. Due to the poor breeding practices of unscrupulous, profit-seeking, back-yard breeders, the normally intelligent and friendly Cocker can turn into a dominating, aggressive dog with severe behavioral problems. Reputable breeders, of course, strive to preserve the best qualities of the breed. Cocker Spaniels range from 13.5 to 15.5 inches at the shoulder and have long coats

Two English Setters, one liver and one black, on either side of their Gordon Setter pal. English Setters are white with markings seen in various colors, while Gordons are black and tan.

The Cockapoo, generated from a Cocker Spaniel and a Miniature Poodle, is the most popular "designer dog" in the world.

A mixed-breed dog of retriever and setter lineage, on the job and showing the skills of his ancestry.

that require regular grooming. Cocker Spaniels can be parti-colored (white with another solid color) or solid-colored, with or without tan points. Common solid colors are black, buff and brown, although others are acceptable.

English Cocker Spaniels (simply called Cocker Spaniels in England, where they are very popular) stand a little taller than the American breed, reaching up to 17 inches at the shoulder and up to 34 pounds in weight. Their muzzles, ears and legs are longer than those of their American counterparts. Their coloring includes blue and brown roan, solid colors, black and tan and black with white (or with tan *and* white). This breed does well with young-

English Springer Spaniels are active sporting dogs that also make wonderful family companions. Guinness enjoys all the comforts of home.

sters and is very adaptable to most living situations; however, they can be headstrong and require consistency and companionship. In Australia English Cockers are commonly crossed with Miniature Poodles to create a delightful mix known as a Spoodle.

English Springer Spaniels are currently very popular hunting dogs. They have lots of energy, talent and intelligence, adapting well to any environment. However, if poorly bred, they can, like Cocker Spaniels, become possessive-aggressive and distrustful of strangers. They stand 19 to 20 inches at the shoulder and weigh 40 to 50 pounds. Their long coats require regular grooming, including some trimming, but should look natural. The most common colors are black and liver, both with white markings; blue and liver roan are also seen. Some black/white and liver/white dogs have tan points over their brows, on their cheeks and on their legs.

The Vizsla is gaining popularity as a pet but is not too often crossed with other breeds. Vizslas may look like hound dogs but are actually part of the Sporting Group due to their pointing and retrieving abilities. They can stand up to 24 inches at the shoulder, making them a medium-to-large breed. Their short coats are burnt orange to light brown in color and their weight ranges from 50 to 60 pounds. These are high-energy dogs that require a lot of exercise and regular obedience training sessions for many years. While they are not often seen within a mixed breed's lineage, it does happen on occasion.

The Weimaraner is often seen in mixes, as the breed has become fairly popular in recent years. With his silver-gray coat and matching gray (sometimes amber) eyes, regal appearance and high energy level, he makes a great companion for an active family that has time to spend working with him. Weimaraners were originally bred for hunting big game. This is a large breed that can stand up to a maximum of 28 inches tall and can weight upward of 75 pounds, depending on height.

HOUND GROUP

Hounds were some of the first known hunting dogs developed. They have been specialized into trackers for locating prey and are rarely used in flushing, retrieving and pointing. Hounds will often follow a trail regardless of any distraction, even that of their owners calling them to come. These breeds can be energetic, bold and stubborn, a combination that often means "difficult to train." It is rare, however, to find an aggressive dog in this group. All hounds require consistent and patient training and must learn at an early age to always come when called, regardless of an interesting scent (something hound owners will attest is easier said than done).

One of the most well-known scenthounds, the Basset Hound is a true charmer... just look into those eyes!

Divided into two categories, hounds hunt by scent or by sight. The most commonly encountered hounds include the Beagle, Dachshund, Basset Hound, Greyhound and several breeds of coonhound. Other less commonly seen hounds, though certainly recognizable, are the Bloodhound, Whippet, Afghan Hound, Rhodesian Ridgeback, Basenji, Borzoi, Foxhound, Ibizan Hound, Irish Wolfhound, Norwegian Elkhound, Otterhound, Saluki and Scottish Deerhound.

The Basset Hound is one of the more popular scenthound breeds and is often seen in many mixed-breed combinations. With his very long ears, short legs and long nose, a Basset can worm his way into anyone's heart. However, Bassets can be very stubborn, willful and difficult to train, but will easily train their people. Bassets have loose skin and short coats that vary from white with black, brown or tan patches and freckles to tan with black patches. They average 14 inches at the shoulder and 40 to 55 pounds. If you see a mixed-breed dog with short legs and long ears, it's a good bet that he's part Basset Hound.

Also scenthounds, Beagles are also very popular and seen even more often in mixes than Basset Hounds. The reason is that many people who hunt with Beagles lose them in the woods and then go home, hoping that their dogs will turn up a few days later. Meanwhile, their Beagles are having a grand time with the neighborhood canines! Beagles can be stubborn but are very intelligent. Once they catch a scent, however, there's not much that will distract them from pursuing it. They come in two size varieties: 13-inch, with an average weight of

19 pounds, and 15-inch, with an average weight of 25 pounds. Beagles' short coats are usually colored in combinations of white, shades of brown and black, some-times with freckles. They have droopy ears and straight tails. Their personalities range from inquisitive and friendly to demanding and phobia-prone.

All of the coonhound breeds are great scent-hunting partners or companions for people who enjoy the outdoors. Some might be timid around strangers and/or aggressive with other dogs. They are high-energy dogs, requiring a lot of exercise. They stand from 21 to 27 inches at the shoulders and weigh anywhere from 40 to 90 pounds depending on breed, sex and height. Like the Basset Hound, coonhounds have loose skin and short, coarse coats. They all have long ears and long tails with heavy bone structure. The Black and Tan, Redbone and Plott are registered by the AKC, but there are other very popular coonhounds, such as the Bluetick, English and Treeing Walker, that are not yet registered with the AKC but are recognized by the United Kennel Club (UKC). The AKC and the UKC both offer coonhound-only performance events.

Bloodhounds are mild-mannered scenting dogs that are renowned for their tracking abili-ties. They are generally great with people, but can be aggressive with

Beagles are true pack dogs and are seen in two sizes, both shown here.

other dogs. They can be stubborn and strong, requiring persistent, patient human companions. This breed stands up to 27 inches at the shoulder and can weigh up to 110 pounds—a very large dog, indeed. They are loose-skinned with short coats in either black and tan, liver and tan or solid red. Some are flecked with white spots or have some white on their chests, feet or tail tips. Their faces are wrinkly and the jowls hang low. Their ears are very long and, when pulled forward, reach beyond their noses, similar to the Basset Hound. Though the breed is not uncommon, it is rarely seen in mixes.

Dachshunds are very popular and their attributes can often be recognized among those of mixed-breed dogs. Their short legs, long bodies, long pointy snouts and

The Bloodhound is a large scenthound whose scenting ability is legendary.

silky ears are unmistakable. They are intelligent, stubborn and clever. They are quick to learn their owners' weaknesses and exploit them to their own advantage. They come in three coat varieties—longhaired, shorthaired and wirehaired. There are also two sizes: Standard, at 9 inches tall and weighing 16 to 32 pounds; and Miniature, at 5 inches tall and under 11 pounds in weight. Common Dachshund colors are solid red, chocolate, black and blue, some with tan points, and the attractive dappled pattern.

From the scenthounds, we move on to the sighthounds. Greyhounds have been hunting dogs since their development in ancient Egypt. As a sighthound, and the fastest dog alive, the Greyhound has been used in the dog-racing industry and often discarded when past its prime, usually at rather young ages. Fortunately, there are many active organizations promoting the adoption of retired racing dogs. The Greyhound is a very sensitive

A hound fancier's delight, this adorable Black and Tan Coonhound pup has the signature scenthound traits of long ears and loose skin.

Smooth Dachshunds in two of the breed's color patterns: solid red and black and tan.

The Greyhound is perhaps the most well known of the sighthounds. He is a tall, lean dog, renowned for his keen eyes and quickness.

breed and generally easy to train. Retired racers can present certain challenges, but most are sweet and docile.

Greyhounds are large, standing up to 30 inches at the shoulder and weighing up to 70 pounds. Their long legs, lean frames and slender necks hold small heads with long pointed snouts. They are extremely aerodynamic. Their short coats come in a variety of colors, including white, gray, fawn, black, brindle and patched. Their ears fold back against their heads, but perk to half-mast when the dogs are interested in something.

Rhodesian Ridgebacks are gaining in popularity and may be seen sometimes in mixes. The ridge along the back is a dead giveaway! The Ridgeback's short coat ranges from light tan to dark red, sometimes with white on the chest. His ears hang down and his eye color ranges from brownish yellow to dark brown. The breed can stand up to 27 inches at the shoulder and can weigh upwards of 75 pounds. Ridgebacks are high-energy dogs that require consistent training and lots of exercise.

Whippets are similar in build and appearance to Greyhounds, only smaller. Whippets stand around 22 inches at the shoulder and weigh 24 to 36 pounds. They can be timid with people they don't know and should be obedience-trained to help build their confidence and control over their sighthound instincts. They too are high-energy dogs that need lots of exercise. Their short coats are varied in color, as all colors and patterns are acceptable. They have large dark eyes and long slender tails.

WORKING GROUP
These breeds were developed for a variety of tasks from guarding, herding and pulling to carrying loads and search-and-rescue. They can adapt to any temperature and

exhibit extreme intelligence and working abilities. Working-breed dogs can make great pets if fully integrated into their family packs. However, if left alone for long periods, chained up or constantly kenneled without any interaction, they can become dangerously aggressive. Some of these breeds were originally bred as fighting dogs, making them risky to have around children or small pets.

Among the most popular dogs in the Working Group are the Boxer, Rottweiler, Siberian Husky, Doberman Pinscher and Great Dane. Some other relatively common breeds in this group are the Mastiff, St. Bernard, Akita, Newfoundland, Bullmastiff, Great Pyrenees and Bernese Mountain Dog. The less common breeds in this category are the Alaskan Malamute, a breed considerably larger than the Siberian Husky, with which it is sometimes mistaken; the Giant and Standard Schnauzers, the latter being less common; the massive corded Komondor; the handsome all-white Kuvasz; the versatile, curly-coated Portuguese Water Dog and the solid-white, long-coated, ever-smiling Samoyed.

Boxers are very popular dogs and often seen within the mixed-breed contingent. Their short muzzles, wide jaws, large brown eyes and broad foreheads are unmistakable. Boxers have muscular bodies, long legs, short coats and droopy ears (if not cropped). They can stand up to 25 inches at the shoulder and weigh 65 to 75 pounds. Their coats are usually

A handsome Rhodesian Ridgeback/Bull Terrier mix.

The Boxer is a popular pet whose roots are in Germany as a working dog.

The Samoyed is a large white spitz breed, classified in the Working Group and known for his signature "Sammy smile."

fawn or brindle with varying amounts of white. They are often stubborn but, if taught early and consistently, make great pets for just about anyone.

Rottweilers became very popular in a short period of time. Not too many years ago, the average American had never even heard of a Rottweiler! They are large, muscular dogs, predominantly black in color with rust-colored or reddish markings on certain points of the body. When well bred, properly socialized and trained, they are loyal and well behaved. If allowed to mature without guidance, with their powerful bodies, strong jaw power and dominating personalities, they can become a nuisance and even dangerous.

The black and tan Rottweiler has an impressive head and stocky build.

This breed can stand up to 27 inches at the shoulder and weigh 85 to 115 pounds. Their ears hang

down and their eyes are brown. Due to its phenomenal surge in popularity (and all of the mass breeding and profiteering that accompany meeting such a demand), the breed has suffered in health and temperament as its "stock" climbed up the AKC registration-statistics list. Today, Rottweiler blood is very commonly found in many mixed-breed dogs.

The Doberman Pinscher is another popular breed often seen within mixed breeds. Due to its high popularity, the Doberman has been plagued by poor breeding practices, which can result in skeletal, organ and/or other disorders in offspring. Far too often, they are left sexually intact and unattended, leading to "accidental" pairings.

The Doberman Pinscher is an intelligent, active dog that is sensitive and eager to work. The breed's short coat comes in black, red, silver/gray (called blue) and fawn (called Isabella) with rust highlights over the eyes and on the cheeks, chest and legs. Grooming-wise, they are easy to maintain. If

not cropped, their ears hang down. Pure-bred Dobermans in the US have cropped tails, as do Boxers and some other breeds, but they are not born in this manner, so few mixes will have their tails cropped on purpose. Dobermans can grow to 28 inches at the shoulder and will weigh 60 to 85 pounds when in good condition.

The Doberman Pinscher is another handsome German contribution to the world of working dogs.

The Great Dane is another large breed that, surprisingly, is often seen within mixes. If the mixed-breed dog stands over 28 inches at the shoulder and weighs over 120 pounds with short fur, black muzzle and droopy ears, there's a good chance that he's part Great Dane. Minimum heights for Danes are 30 inches for males and 28 inches for females, with taller heights preferred. They can be dominant in a sneaky sort of way. They don't confront, they insinu-ate, gradually gaining the alpha position without their people real-izing it. Their short, easy-to-main-tain coats come in brindle, fawn, black, silver (blue), harlequin and mantle, the latter two being black and white patterns. Merle is seen

as well, although this color is not acceptable for showing. All-white or mostly white Danes usually have some degree of deafness.

Siberian Huskies are very popular dogs. They are beautiful, with alert expressions, thick coats, upright ears and piercing eyes. Common colors are white with gray, black or rust, but any color from white to black is allowed. Their eyes are seen in shades of

A combination of two working breeds, this is a Siberian Husky/Rottweiler mix.

A Great Dane from Germany, the breed's homeland. Many European dogs have natural ears, while Danes in the US can be seen with either cropped or natural ears.

The Akita is the largest of the spitz breeds from Japan.

brown and blue, sometimes one of each. They stand up to 23.5 inches at the shoulder and weigh up to 60 pounds. They can be mischievous and difficult to train, but always lively, thus requiring a lot of exercise. Husky attributes are commonly found within mixed-breed dogs, and many working sled dogs are simply Husky crosses (sometimes called Alaskan Huskies or just Huskies).

Akitas, deriving from the spitz breeds of Japan, are large, heavily coated dogs with triangular-shaped heads, small triangular ears and bushy tails that curl over their backs. They can be strong-willed and, if not socialized at an early age, aggressive with other dogs. They stand up to 28 inches at the shoulder and weigh between 75 and 110 pounds. Their colors include fawn, white with brown or black patches, brindle, solid white, black and more.

The Bernese Mountain Dog is not seen in many mixed breeds. The breed has a mostly black coat that is long and slightly wavy, with white on the chest, neck and muzzle, a blaze between the eyes and rust points. Berners are very gentle dogs that can be timid if not socialized at an early age. They stand up to 27.5 inches at the shoulder and can weigh up to 110 pounds. Their ears hang down and their eyes are dark brown. It may be rare to see this lineage within a mix, but not unheard of.

Bullmastiffs may be docile but, once riled, do not back down easily. After all, they were developed as watchdogs for large estates in England. Bullmastiffs are very easy to maintain with their short coats and low energy levels, but are often difficult to train. They can stand up to 27 inches at the shoulder and weigh a hefty 130 pounds if well muscled. They have some similarities to the Boxer, coming in fawn and brindle (Bullmastiffs can also be red), with ears that hang down, somewhat shortened muzzles and wrinkly foreheads. Often, a pet-quality Boxer may be mistaken for a skinny Bullmastiff, and either can be seen in a mixed breed.

Great Pyrenees are large, heavily coated, white dogs that stand up to 32 inches at the shoulder and can weigh over 100 pounds. If not socialized at a young age, they can be aggressive with other dogs and hard-headed about listening to their owners. Great Pyrenees have dark brown eyes and thick ears that hang down. These are not common pets and therefore are not often seen within the attributes of a mixed breed.

Once used as war dogs in the Roman legions, Mastiffs (sometimes called English Mastiffs) are *large.* They stand about 30 inches at the shoulder and weigh 170 to 200 pounds. This is a fairly good-natured dog but, if not properly socialized, tends to be aggressive with other dogs. Mastiffs' ears fold over, wrinkles adorn their faces and they have long jowls. Their short coats can be fawn, brindle or apricot with dark muzzles, eyes and ears.

Newfoundlands are large teddy bears, with long, thick coats that can be black, black and white, brown or gray. The Newf's triangular ears hang down and his eyes are dark brown. This is a hardy dog that was initially utilized for pulling carts. The breed is gentle, easy to train and very sociable. Newfoundlands stand up to 28 inches at the shoulder and can weigh 150 pounds when fully grown. Given the responsible

The Mastiff is a giant breed with a gentle temperament by nature.

owners of most Newfs, this breed is uncommonly encountered in mixed breeds.

St. Bernards come in two varieties: longhaired, the more common, and shorthaired. This large breed with droopy eyes and jowls can weigh upwards of 160 pounds. Minimum height is 27.5

The Bullmastiff, despite his large size, can be a good house dog because of his relatively low activity level.

A longhaired St. Bernard. Raised by monks in the snowy Swiss Alps, the breed's search-and-rescue ability is legendary.

inches for males and 25.5 inches for females. Their coats usually have reddish brown to tan patches on white, but sometimes are seen in brindle on white. Although quiet in the house, they do require lots of outdoor exercise and consistent obedience training. St. Bernards have dark brown eyes, ears that hang down and thick, straight tails. This breed is usually carefully bred, but can occasionally be recognized within a mixed-breed dog's attributes.

TERRIER GROUP

Bred for hunting small game such as rodents, rabbits and fox, terriers are tenacious, high-energy, rebellious to authority and more aggressive than any other group. When riled, they do not back down easily. However, they do learn quickly and, if given proper guidance, socialization and obedience training, make great pets.

Terriers are commonly seen within mixed-breed bloodlines. The most popular breeds are the Jack Russell Terrier (now officially called the Parson Russell Terrier by the AKC), the American Pit Bull Terrier (recognized by the United Kennel Club) as well as its AKC counterpart, the American Staffordshire Terrier, and the closely related Staffordshire Bull Terrier, the Miniature Schnauzer and the West Highland White, Fox, Cairn, Scottish, Airedale, Soft Coated Wheaten, Rat and Bull Terriers. The less common breeds include the Border, Kerry Blue, Welsh, Australian, Bedlington, Dandie Dinmont, Lakeland, Manchester, Norfolk, Norwich, Sealyham and Skye Terriers.

Airedale Terriers are the largest terriers in the group, standing 23 inches at the shoulder and weighing up to 60 pounds. Their wiry, curly coats are coarse and require regular clipping to maintain cleanliness and neatness. They are predominantly tan with black or gray saddles over their backs, forward-folding ears, dark eyes and black noses. This is a bold, headstrong breed that requires proper training and socialization.

The Airedale is the largest of the Terrier Group. Pictured here are a male (the larger of the two) and female.

American Pit Bull/American Staffordshire Terriers are powerful dogs with heavily muscled bodies. Size in this breed varies considerably, though the AKC AmStaffs should stand only up to 19 inches at the shoulder and weigh up to about 65 pounds. Some lines of Pit Bull can be larger, though the smaller dogs are preferred by most breeders. They all have short coats that can be seen in a wide range of color, including fawn, brindle, patched or black. Their ears naturally fold over, but are often cropped to stand up straight. Their jaws are powerful, making their bites deadly. These dogs must have early socialization with people and other dogs as well as daily obedience training. Pit Bulls have a notorious reputation, but properly bred, raised and trained Pit Bulls make loving and reward-

The Staffordshire Bull Terrier bears resemblance to the American Staffordshire Terrier, but is a shorter, stockier dog.

ing companions, as those who know the true Pit Bull will attest. The Pit Bull-Rottweiler cross has become fairly common, as have the "Bandog" crosses (male Pit Bull/female Mastiff, Neapolitan Mastiff or Bullmastiff).

Bull Terriers, known for their egg-shaped heads, are medium-sized, short-coated dogs. They are usually solid white or solid-colored with or without white markings, the latter particularly seen in brindle. Their large Roman noses, small eyes and upright ears give them comical expressions, often matching their clownish personalities. Their ears fold over, but prick up halfway when alert. They stand up to 24 inches at the shoulders and, like AmStaffs, are heavily muscled, sometimes weighing as much as 80 pounds. Miniature Bull Terriers stand between 10 and 14 inches tall, weighing up to 33 pounds. Bull Terriers are often mistaken for the American Staffordshires/Pit Bulls, but are clearly not the same. There

The American Staffordshire Terrier is a handsome, powerful dog. When raised properly, he is a friendly and affectionate family companion.

The Bull Terrier is a charming and unique breed in both looks and personality.

are obvious differences in head shape and more. These dogs must receive proper training and regular exercise.

The ever-popular West Highland White Terrier is not as stubborn as many of the other terrier breeds but, if not socialized and trained, can be just as scrappy with strangers. As the breed's name implies, Westies are white. They have dark eyes, black lips and black noses. Their small triangular ears prick upward and they stand around 10 to 11 inches at the shoulder, weighing up to 20 pounds.

This adorable mixed-breed pup comes from a Bull Terrier sire and Staffordshire Bull Terrier dam.

Cairn Terriers are small dogs, originally developed for hunting small mammals in difficult terrain. They are assertive, high-energy dogs that can be aggressive with other animals if not raised with them. Their wiry coats can be seen in almost anything but white, including wheaten, red, brindle, silver and black. Their small triangular ears and short straight tails are upright most of the time. Their hazel eyes miss nothing.

Miniature Schnauzers are very popular, for they fit into any environment. They accept new people and other animals fairly easily, and they learn quickly. At no more than 14 inches tall and averaging 15 pounds in weight, they make great dogs for those living in apartments or condominiums. However, they do have a lot of energy and require regular exercise. Their coats are wiry, but they grow in long and require regular clipping. Their colors range from silver gray to solid black. If the ears are not cropped, they fold over forward. Pure-breds have docked tails.

The Rat Terrier has long been one of the US's favorite companion dogs, though it is not recognized by the AKC. The United Kennel Club (which also recognizes the Pit Bull) does recognize the breed. It has a similar appearance to a short-legged Parson Russell Terrier with a broad, slightly domed head. Rat Terriers are white in color, usually with one or two other colors (such as tan, brown, black, red, lemon and more). Rat Terriers come in two sizes, the Miniature variety (not exceeding 13 inches) and the Standard variety (13 to 18 inches).

Scottish Terriers, although small, have huge personalities. In fact, they think they are big dogs that can take over the world. Independent, stubborn and sometimes aggressive with other dogs, Scotties can be difficult to train

Two longtime favorites of the Terrier Group: the Scottie and the Westie.

and are easily distracted. They stand around 10 inches at the shoulder and weigh, on average, around 20 pounds. Their ears prick up and their dark eyes are always alert. Their long coats are predominantly black, but brindle and wheaten are also accepted colors in the breed.

Fox Terriers are great in the field but sometimes make difficult

pets, for they have such extreme energy levels that it is difficult to keep them quiet. They are bold, fearless and playful. The Smooth Fox Terrier has a short coat, stands around 15 inches at the shoulder and can weigh around 16 to 18 pounds. The Wire Fox Terrier is the same size, but with a wiry coat that varies in length on different parts of the body. Their coats are predominantly white, often with brown or black (or combination thereof) patches. Their ears fold forward and their eyes are dark. These dogs must be trained or else they will get into plenty of mischief.

The media have made Jack Russell Terriers (Parson Russell

A mix of two popular small breeds: Miniature Schnauzer and Dachshund.

The Rat Terrier is not recognized by the American Kennel Club but is a very popular breed in the US.

The Fox Terrier is seen in Smooth and Wire varieties; the Wire Fox Terrier is pictured here.

Terriers) very popular. Unfortunately, the shows featuring these dogs do not depict their true nature. They are terriers in every sense of the word: raucous, noisy, aggressive with strange dogs and highly energetic. They are also very intelligent and, if given an opportunity, they will run with it. Don't let their cuteness fool you. These dogs *must* have obedience training. Most stand around 12 to 14 inches and weigh around 15 pounds although there is some variation in size and type. The coat is either broken or smooth,

The Jack Russell Terrier, now known as the Parson Russell Terrier, is active and feisty, a true terrier.

usually white with tan and/or black patches and freckles. Their ears fold forward, although some dogs have ears that stand up.

Soft Coated Wheaten Terriers are very gentle and more readily approachable than most of the other terrier breeds. They do have a lot of energy but, if given the chance to exercise, are quiet house dwellers. They are medium-sized dogs, standing up to 19 inches tall and weighing around 40 pounds. Their smallish ears fold over and down, and their dark brown eyes convey a kind expression. Their long wheat-colored coats are silky and wavy, requiring frequent attention or else they will be prone to knots.

Not too common in the US but quite popular in the UK, Border Terriers are very adaptable and love to work. Their wiry coats are short and usually shades of tan or reddish brown with dark-tipped hairs. They have dark brown eyes and ears that fold forward. They stand up to 15 inches at the shoulder; weight ranges from about 12 to 18 pounds, depending on working conditions. They are very responsive to obedience training, provided the approach is patient and not harsh. They do enjoy crawling into tight places, due to their instinctual desire to hunt small animals.

Recognizable to many dog lovers are the Norfolk Terrier and Norwich Terrier, once considered a single breed. Indeed, they are very similar in size, coloring and personality. They originated in England as vermin hunters, giving them their feisty, bold personalities. The only way a novice can distinguish between the two is that the Norfolk has folded ears and the Norwich has upright ears, though there are other differences. They stand 10 inches at the shoulder and weigh around 12 pounds, with short, wiry coats that vary from reddish brown to wheaten, with black-tipped hairs, black and tan or grizzle.

TOY GROUP

Most toy breeds are pampered house pets, rarely left outdoors unsupervised. Nonetheless, toy-breed crosses do occur, sometimes on purpose, and some of these intentional crosses have become fairly popular. You will need to know if your "Heinz 57" might

The Norwich and Norfolk Terriers resemble each other closely; the main distinction is made by the Norwich's (shown here) prick ears.

have some toy blood in him.

Most of the toy breeds were developed from the other major dog groups, their behaviors similar to the breeds from which they were derived. Toys acclimate easily to any environment and, due to their small size, do not require much space to receive proper exercise. Most of these breeds do have house-training problems. However, this is due more to their being spoiled than to their own stubbornness, although that can be part of the excuse. If not trained, toy breeds tend to bark excessively and are easily aggravated if they do not get what they want.

The most common toy breeds seen in mixes are Toy Poodles, Pomeranians, Pekingese, Shih Tzu, Yorkshire Terriers and Pugs. Other very popular toy breeds include the Chihuahua, Maltese, Miniature Pinscher, Papillon, Cavalier King Charles Spaniel, Toy Fox Terrier and Italian Greyhound. Each of these breeds has recognizable char-

The Soft Coated Wheaten Terrier is softer in coat and personality than most other terrier breeds.

The smallest dog in this group portrait is the Toy Poodle, hanging out with the "big dogs."

This Yorkie mix is larger and shorter-coated than a pure-bred Yorkshire Terrier, but he does have the breed's blue and tan coloration.

most popular of the toy breeds. They are intelligent, making training easy, but can be reserved with strangers. They have ears that hang down, dark eyes and curly coats that need regular grooming. They are usually of solid coloration and can be seen in just about any color and shade. The Toy Poodle as well as the medium-sized Poodle variety, known as the Miniature Poodle (part of the Non-Sporting Group), are commonly bred to various toy breeds like the Pomeranian, Pekingese, Yorkshire Terrier and Pug, creating such crosses as the Pomapoo, Peke-a-poo, Yorkiepoo and Pugapoo.

Pekingese are easy to spot with their dark, short muzzles and bulbous eyes. Their ears hang down and are covered in silky long fur. They stand 9 inches at the shoulder and should not weigh over 14 pounds, making them ideal for small homes in a variety of environments. Their long coats can be seen in any color or pattern. These dogs need to be trained or they can become assertive.

acteristics, making it easy to know if your mixed-breed dog does indeed have some toy-breed blood in him. The lesser-known toy breeds include the Affenpinscher, Brussels Griffon, English Toy Spaniel, Japanese Chin, Toy Manchester Terrier and Silky Terrier. The breeding and ownership of these breeds is rather exclusive, so it would indeed be a rarity to see these breeds in the lineage of a mixed-breed dog.

The Toy Poodle, the smallest variety of Poodle, is among the

The Pekingese is a charming, short-faced, abundantly coated toy with origins in China.

Pomeranians are little balls of fluff. They stand only 7 inches at the shoulder and weigh no more than 7 pounds, mostly fur. Their abundant double coats stand out from the body along with their upright ears. Their coats come in a variety of colors from white to black, sable and parti-color with patches. These dogs can be demanding and need obedience training or they will easily take over the household. Don't let their small size fool you!

Many poorly bred Poms are larger than the sizes indicated by the AKC and can stand as tall as 12 to 14 inches. These large dogs should not be confused with the European breed known as the German Spitz, from which the Pomeranian descends.

Pugs are easy to care for and train, but are very prone to problems with extreme weather conditions (such as difficulty breathing in heat and humidity) due to their brachycephalic skull shape (relatively broad and short). Their muzzles are usually black, and they have dark bulbous eyes and short ears that fold over. They stand up to 11 inches at the shoulder and can weigh up to 18 pounds, although some can be prone to obesity and weigh more. Their short coats can be silver or apricot-fawn with a black face, some with a black stripe down their backs, or solid black.

Shih Tzu are happy, easygoing

The Pomeranian is a delightful little dog with a magnificent full coat; he is the smallest of the German spitz breeds.

dogs that love to play. Easy to train and responsive, these toy dogs are great companions, easily winning over many hearts. They stand between 8 and 11 inches tall and weigh a mere 9 to 16 pounds. Their long, silky coats are acceptable in any color or combination. They require much attention to grooming, especially if kept in full coat.

Yorkshire Terriers are bold, active dogs that require a lot of exercise and early socialization. Yorkies are born with gold and

The Pug shares the short muzzle and country of origin with the Pekingese.

black coats, which turn to steel blue and tan as they age. Their coats are long and silky, requiring regular brushing. They have perky expressions, upright ears and dark eyes. Standing only 9 inches at the shoulder and weighing no more than 7 pounds, they are easy to take along while traveling.

Chihuahuas have been immortalized through media exposure, most notably the Taco Bell™ dog. These well-known favorites are not

accurate representations of the breed, however. Most Chihuahuas have much smaller ears and rounded heads. The longhaired Chihuahua in particular tends to be smaller in stature with a short neck, small ears and short nose. The shorthaired variety is more similar to the popular Taco Bell™ dog, but normally does not have such a slim, long-legged body and huge ears. Overall, these dogs are easy to train and love people, but can be a little feisty. They stand

only 5 inches at the shoulders and weigh a mere 5 to 6 pounds. Their coats are seen in a veritable rainbow of colors and patterns.

The Toy Fox Terrier ranks among the most popular toy breeds in the US, though he is a newcomer to the AKC's ranks. The United Kennel Club has registered the breed for decades and there are thousands of them around. The

dog stands about 9 to 11 inches in height and is short-coated. In color, they are white with either black, tan, black and tan or chocolate and tan markings. They are recognizable by their erect, pointed ears, set high on their elegant narrow heads. They are sweet, intelligent and most resourceful little dogs. Some lines can be mistaken for small Rat Terriers, though the earset should give them away.

The Cavalier King Charles Spaniel is one of the most docile and friendly of the small dog breeds. He has lots of energy and is easily trained. Standing only 12 to 13 inches at the shoulder and weighing 15 to 18 pounds, the Cavalier King Charles Spaniel has a medium-length silky coat that is seen in four varieties. The Blenheim coloration is white with chestnut-red markings. Tricolor Cavaliers are white with black markings and rich tan points. Black and Tan refers to mostly black with chestnut markings similar to those of the Tricolor. The Ruby is the solid red variety. A Cavalier's fur is feathered at the chest, legs, ears and tail. His long ears hang down, much like a Cocker Spaniel's, and he has dark brown eyes and a black nose.

Maltese are long-coated, white-haired, lively dogs with independent personalities. Owners must resist the temptation to overly pamper these dogs or else they

In the Maltese, the fluffy white puppy coat is replaced with long, straight, silky hair as the dog matures.

will take over the household! Their silky ears hang down, their gentle eyes are dark brown and their noses are black. They stand 8 inches and can weigh up to 7 pounds.

The Miniature Pinscher looks very much like his taller cousin, the Doberman Pinscher, but the Min Pin is more independent and bold. He can be willful and an excessive barker. Miniature

A handsome Cavalier with tricolor markings.

Big wins in the show ring have brought the Papillon into the public eye. The breed's name means "butterfly" in French, after the shape of his ears.

Pinschers stand up to 12.5 inches tall, weigh around 10 pounds and have short easy-care coats that come in solid red, stag red (red mixed with black hairs), black with rust points and chocolate with rust points. If not cropped, their ears fold over. Their eyes are usually dark brown.

With their sweet faces, huge ears and becoming personalities, it's easy to see why the Papillon is enjoying a resurgence in popularity. Papillons, derived from smart spaniels, are the most intelligent and gentle of all of the Toy breeds; however, they require early socialization to become accepting of new places and people. Standing no more than 11 inches tall and weighing no more than 10 pounds,

The Min Pin has garnered the nickname "King of Toys," thanks to his commanding personality in a tiny-sized body.

Papillons are ideal for any living situation. Their silky coats are seen in white with patches of any color. Sometimes their butterfly ears hang down (known as the Phalene variety), but most Papillons have upright ears.

NON-SPORTING GROUP

A fair number of popular breeds are classified as Non-Sporting. Like the toy breeds, these breeds are related to breeds in other groups and exhibit similar characteristics. The most popular members of the group are the Miniature and Standard Poodles, Boston Terrier, Bulldog, Bichon

Frise, Lhasa Apso, Chinese Shar-Pei, American Eskimo Dog, Dalmatian and Chow Chow. Other breeds in the group include the Shiba Inu, Finnish Spitz, French Bulldog, Keeshond, Schipperke, Tibetan Spaniel and Tibetan Terrier. The breeds discussed here are those Non-Sporting breeds most commonly found in mixed breeds.

Of course, the font of all "Poos," the Poodles are among the most popular breeds entangled in mixed marriages. This fact can be supported by many good reasons. Miniature Poodles are the easiest of the Poodle breeds to live with. The Miniature and Standard Poodles both love to please, but they need ample exercise. They are infinitely intelligent and almost humanlike in their ability to solve problems. Their coats are curly, and owners must commit to grooming and coat maintenance. All of the Poodle breeds vary in color, and almost anything between white and black (within reason) can be seen. The AKC does not permit parti-colored Poodles to compete in shows, though these unique-looking dogs can be seen around the world. Topped with a pompom, the Poodle's tail is normally docked.

Miniature Poodles stand from 10 up to and including 15 inches at the shoulder and can weigh 12 to 14 pounds. Standard Poodles stand higher, at over 15 inches at

A handsome black Miniature Poodle in full show coat. For pet owners, don't dismay, as most pet Poodles are kept in the easy-to-care-for pet trim.

The Standard Poodle is a strong, athletic, intelligent dog...perfect for those who want all of the breed's glowing attributes in a larger-sized dog.

the shoulder, and can weigh up to 60 pounds. The Standard Poodle, developed to be a hard-working duck-hunting dog, requires more exercise than his smaller brethren and will thrive with a consistent training regimen and plenty to keep him challenged.

A "powderpuff" of a purebred, the solid-white Bichon Frise is a smallish dog, standing only 9 to 12 inches at the shoulder and weighing 12 pounds. Bichons have ears that hang down, dark brown eyes and white medium-length coats that are very curly and soft, resembling that of a Poodle. Show Bichons are sculpted to the extreme in the US, though in

The Bichon Frise is known for being one of the friendliest, happiest breeds around.

distinct with their brachycephalic heads, upright ears and short tails. Bostons have short fur that is black or brindle with white around the collar, face, legs and feet. Their weight varies and they can weigh up to 25 pounds, making them compact and ideal for city or suburban living. Their energy level is manageable, provided they receive regular walks.

Europe they are a bit more natural-looking. Occasionally a puppy will have some cream or apricot shadings, which disappear with maturity. Bichons are energetic little dogs that can easily wrap their owners around their paws with their loving, outgoing nature. They are true "people dogs."

Boston Terriers are very

The solid white, thickly coated American Eskimo Dog is a popular pet, for the breed is typically friendly and playful. They can be somewhat independent, but do respond well to obedience training. With triangular upright ears, tails that curl over their backs and dark brown eyes, these descendants of the German Spitz come in three size varieties: Toy, standing 9 to 12 inches and weighing 5 to 7 pounds; Miniature, standing 12 to 15 inches and weighing 10 to 20 pounds; and Standard, standing 15 to 19 inches and weighing 25 to 35 pounds.

The "American Gentleman," the Boston Terrier was born in the USA, a dapper fellow in his black and white tuxedo.

Bulldogs are sweet, peaceful (except while sleeping, because they snore) and somewhat stubborn. They have wide-set bodies with short folded-over ears, brachycephalic heads and short glossy coats that come in a variety of colors including white with patches, brindle and reddish brown to fawn. They stand around 15 inches at the shoulder and can weigh a hefty 50 or more pounds. Due to poor breeding practices, many Bulldogs inherit poor temperaments and can be aggressive with people and other dogs.

Chow Chows are very commonly mixed with other breeds, for they are a fairly popular breed. They tend to be devoted to mainly one person and shy around strangers. Some can be aggressive toward other dogs or people if not socialized at an early age. Their thick coats, lion faces and blue-black tongues are unmistakable, as are their poufy tails that curl over their backs when alerted or happy. They stand up to 20 inches at the shoulder and can weigh 60 to 70 pounds. This can be a difficult breed to train for an inexperienced owner.

Recognizable from 100 yards, Dalmatians are high-energy dogs with short black- or liver-spotted coats. They stand no more than 24 inches at the shoulder and can weigh 65 to 70 pounds. Their ears hang down, and they have long muzzles and dark brown or blue eyes. Bred originally to run alongside carriages, this breed has much stamina. Dalmatians require consistent obedience training and lots of exercise.

Lhasa Apsos are popular small dogs that pack a lot of punch for their size. In the UK, they are categorized with the Toy breeds. Independent, bold and playful, they will easily take control if allowed. Lhasas have straight long coats, short noses and dark eyes.

The Bulldog is a true charmer with a short muzzle, facial wrinkling and a stocky, heavy body.

Their coat colors include reddish brown, golden brown, honey, white, gray, brown, black, particolored and other shades. Their ears hang down and are heavily feathered with fur. When excited, their tails curl over their backs.

Chinese Shar-Pei have been bred for wrinkles. Their personalities range from serious and quiet

The Chow is commonly seen in mixed breeds. Purple spotting on a mixed-breed dog's tongue often points to some Chow in his lineage.

Who doesn't recognize the Dalmatian? This energetic spotted breed needs plenty of activity to keep him happy.

to very pushy and dominating. Their coats can be either very harsh and short or smooth. Their colors range from cream to black and almost every color in between. Their large heads have thick lips, big mouths, tiny ears that fold forward and, as in Chow Chows, blue-black tongues. Shar-Pei stand up to 20 inches at the shoulder

The Lhasa Apso is classified as a Toy in some countries. Although small, this is a hardy, substantial dog.

and can weigh up to 60 pounds. This breed became very popular in the 1980s and thus has become easily recognizable. Shar-Pei traits are usually easy to spot in mixed breeds.

HERDING GROUP

These are generally known as the most intelligent and trainable of all breeds. Herding breeds also have high energy levels and require lots of stimulation. These types of dogs do not always work well in homes with young children, for they have a tendency to race after running youngsters, as though herding sheep, and accidentally knock them down.

Some of the breeds in this group are extremely popular as pets and therefore seen within many mixed-breed dogs. The German Shepherd Dog is the top contender for the Don Juan of the Herding Group. In fact, at least 40% of all mixed breeds have German Shepherd Dog or Labrador Retriever in them. Other popular herders include the Collie, Border Collie, Pembroke Welsh Corgi, Shetland Sheepdog, Australian Shepherd and Old English Sheepdog. Less populous breeds in the group include the Australian Cattle Dog, Bearded Collie, Belgian Malinois, Belgian Sheepdog, Belgian Tervuren, Bouvier des Flandres, Briard, Puli and Cardigan Welsh Corgi.

German Shepherd Dogs have been extremely popular ever since the days of the famous Rin Tin Tin. These dogs require mental and physical exercise as well as regular training regimens. They thrive on having a job to do. Their dense coats are usually black with tan, golden tan with black, gray sable with black-tipped hairs or solid black. Some are solid white, although this color is not acceptable for American Kennel Club showing. German Shepherds have upright ears, dark eyes and long, bushy tails. They stand from 22 to 26 inches at the shoulder and can weigh up to 100 pounds. The characteristically tan muzzle with "beauty marks" at the cheeks is commonly seen in many dogs of mixed German Shepherd heritage. Able to guard, protect, herd and perform search-and-rescue, this is truly a dog that can do it all, thus the breed's popularity.

The German Shepherd Dog is famous around the world. He's often put to work in police and military roles, but this intelligent breed also makes a great family pet for the right owner.

Collies come in two varieties, the Smooth and the Rough, the latter of which is far more popular. Both have similarly gentle personalities and like to please, but can be high-strung. They stand from 22 to 26 inches at the shoulders and can weigh 50 to 75 pounds. Their ears are pricked upward with a forward fold-over at the tip. Many tend to bark when excited. Their coloring ranges from sable to blue merle to tricolor, or white with markings in these colors.

The Border Collie is touted by some as the most intelligent of all dog breeds. Although intelligent, the breed can also be difficult to own as a pet. Border Collies need to work. Without an outlet for their energies, Border Collies will choose less positive outlets. Unless properly socialized, some can be

The two varieties of Collie: the more common Rough on the left and the Smooth on the right.

The Border Collie is a very popular dog, touted by many to be one of the smartest canines. He has become known for achieving great success in competitive sports like obedience, agility and flyball.

be cantankerous with other dogs. They are boisterous but stubborn. Their very long coats can be gray, grizzle or blue, with or without white. Old English Sheepdogs have ears that hang down, blending into the coat. They stand up to 22 inches at the shoulder and can weigh 60 to 90 pounds.

Shetland Sheepdogs (often called Shelties) are very popular due to their small stature and beautiful long coats. They resemble the Rough Collie, only smaller, but they are a completely distinct

When you think of "sheepdog," the Old English Sheepdog must spring to mind! Aside from his coat, large size and herding ability, the breed is known for being exuberant and affectionate.

aggressive with strangers or other dogs. Their medium-length coats are primarily seen in black and white, but can be seen in many other colors, too. Their eyes can be dark brown, blue or light brown, depending on coat color, and they have a characteristic intense gaze. Border Collies stand from 18 to 22 inches at the shoulder and can weigh 35 to 50 pounds. Their legs are long and their ears are upright, some with a forward fold-over.

Old English Sheepdogs are very friendly with people, but can

Australian Shepherds in three of the breed's attractive colors: red merle, black (with white markings and tan points) and blue merle.

breed, not "Miniature Collies." They must be trained from a very early age or will easily figure things out and run the show. They can be noisy and high-energy, and they are fast. Shelties can stand anywhere from 13 to 16 inches at the shoulder and weigh up to 18

pounds. Their colors are black, blue merle and sable, marked with white and/or tan.

Australian Shepherds are intelligent, high-energy dogs that love to work. Australian Shepherds were derived from Border Collies, and although the breed's name may indicate a foreign origin, they actually originated in the United States. Their appearance is much like that of their cousin, the Border Collie, only slightly heavier boned, with thicker coats and docked tails. Their coloration includes black and white, red and white, blue and red merle and black and red tricolor. They stand from 18 to 23 inches at the shoulder and can weigh 35 to 65 pounds. Their eye color can be blue, amber, brown or a combination thereof. Their ears fold forward. Some have straight coats, others wavy and thick with feathering at the legs, chest and neck. This breed is gaining in popularity and thus increasing the chances of becoming more frequently seen in mixed breeds.

With proper obedience training, they can tackle any job with ease and pleasure. They are very intelligent, but need to be busy to be happy and well adjusted.

Corgis have large upright ears and very short legs. They are shaped similarly to the Basset Hound, only with upright ears and a smaller bone structure. The Pembroke Welsh Corgi, the more popular of the two, is related to the spitz family and has a shorter back and a more puppylike appearance. The Cardigan Welsh Corgi, the larger of the two and related to the Dachshund, shares the Dachshund's trademark low-slung long back and slightly bowed forelegs. A noticeable difference is the Cardigan's long bushy tail and the Pembroke's almost non-existent tail. Both come in a variety of colors from red to sable to fawn to black, often

While the Sheltie does resemble a smaller-sized Collie, he is a breed all his own.

The Briard is a herder of French origin, recognized by many but not so numerous that he's commonly found in mixed breeds.

The Cardigan Welsh Corgi is the larger of the two Corgi breeds. This breed has a long tail, whereas the Pembroke's tail is barely noticeable.

Labrador Retriever blood can be found in many mixes. This handsome fellow is a Labrador/German Shorthaired Pointer mix.

with white markings, and the Cardigan is also seen in brindle and blue merle. Their coats are primarily short with some feathering at the legs, chest and tail (in Cardigans). Corgis are high-energy, easygoing dogs that are very loving. They may be small, but they have large personalities.

CONCLUSION

Now that you have an idea of what pure-bred dogs look and act like, you will be able to make an educated guess as to the genetic

Can you guess this cutie's parentage? You are correct if you picked Cairn Terrier and Dachshund.

attributes of your mixed-breed dog or a dog that you're considering. Knowing what to expect is half of learning how to live with your new family member. For example, you picked up a puppy at the humane society that is all black with a curly tail, black tongue and bushy, thick coat. It is a good possibility that this might be a

Chow Chow/Labrador Retriever mix. Not only do these physical characteristics point in that direction, but the fact that both are very popular breeds makes this combination very feasible. Maybe you obtained a dog with short legs, longish ears, a long body and a short coat that is predominantly tan with a black saddle, ears and muzzle, and dark eyes. You may well have a Basset Hound/German Shepherd Dog mix.

SELECTING YOUR DOG

Unless you have a friend or neighbor with a litter of puppies or someone you know has to give away a dog, you'll most probably search for a mixed-breed dog at the local animal shelter, humane society or rescue organization. With millions of dogs being euthanized each year, it is best to adopt a dog from one of these sources. Shelters, humane societies and rescue organizations take in stray, abandoned, sick, injured or otherwise homeless dogs that need a second chance in a loving home. They are usually spayed/neutered and given medical treatment before adoption and, in some cases, obedience training and socialization.

Dogs end up in shelters for a number of reasons, most of which are based on human irresponsibility. With the availability of low-cost neuter/spay programs and public education about the benefits of neutering and spaying pets, there really is no viable reason for a person to allow his dog to have an unplanned mating. There is also no excuse for people to obtain a pup or dog and then later give him up if circumstances change or behavior problems arise. These are people who should not own dogs in the first place. This irresponsibility results in millions of euthanized and abused animals each year. While there are many "no-kill" shelters, there also are many that euthanize dogs within a certain time frame, sometimes as little as a week or less, if not reclaimed or adopted. You must realize that, when you bring a dog home, you become responsible for its entire lifetime.

A dog is a social being with feelings and a deep sense of loyalty. Left outside and ignored, this social animal turns into one with major behavioral problems. Think of a person in the same situation—left alone for long periods of time, never taught right from wrong or how to speak, read and write. Dogs need education as much as human beings. An educated dog is one who is at one with his environment. He behaves because he understands. He is relaxed because he trusts his human companions. He is a joy to be around, not a nuisance.

Before obtaining a dog, you should delve deeply into why you want to own a dog in the first place. Think about this simple question: why do you want a pet? Have other family members (like the children) been asking for one? Are you lonely and want some company? You should never get a dog just for the kids. They are not the ones who will be responsible for the dog. You are. You must have the time, be financially able and have the desire to be a doggie parent.

Dogs require a lot of your time. They need house-training, obedience training, visits to the veterinarian and regular exercise. They also cost a lot of money. Although a mixed-breed dog from a shelter or rescue group will cost less initially than a pure-bred, there are still the same expenses for his upkeep, which will be hundreds of dollars annually. Once your adopted canine becomes a member of your household, you must be able to afford providing for his needs, which is a necessity no matter what type of dog you've chosen. All dogs require licenses, veterinary check-ups, yearly inoculations, heartworm preventives and flea preparations, food, equipment, grooming and training. As dogs age, their bodies break down and illnesses can occur. Your dog's veterinary care can amount to thousands of dollars over the course of a single dog's lifetime. Are you willing and able to commit yourself to that?

What happens if you move? Can you take your dog with you? Should you be in the military, where you are moved every year or two, can you confidently say that you can take your dog with you wherever you go? This is usually not the case, for most military personnel spend much of their time overseas, often in places where dogs must be quarantined for a period of time.

Are you planning on starting a family? This is a serious consideration. Do you think it would be fair to a dog to be ignored because all of your time is taken up by young children? Keep in mind that a dog is an eternal child. As puppies, they are similar to toddlers. They get into everything. Thus, puppies must be watched just like human toddlers. Leaving your dog outside in the yard or tied up is not the answer. This

Black and Tan Coonhound mix pup Sadie is having sweet doggie dreams after making a long journey from a shelter in Georgia to her new home in New Jersey.

does not teach him to behave. In fact, it teaches him to misbehave in order to receive some sort of attention. What happens when he barks excessively? You go out and yell at him. This may be negative attention, but to your dog it's better than no attention at all.

Dogs can be properly prepared for new infants, but you must also prepare your children for your dog. Teaching children how to pet, approach and interact with a dog is very important. If this isn't done, you will be putting both the children and the dog in danger. Injuries can occur inadvertently in play to either party. A dog who injures a child, even if by accident, might be deemed as unsuitable to keep as a pet, when in reality all that is needed is adult supervision to make sure that the child and dog treat each other properly.

Another question you should ask yourself is if your home is suitable for your pet. If you are renting an apartment or house, make sure that dogs are allowed. Nothing is worse than obtaining a dog from a shelter and then turning around and giving him back a week later because your landlord said "no." This traumatizes a dog, making him feel even more insecure. If you are obtaining a mixed-breed dog as a puppy, consider that you will not know exactly what size he will be when fully grown. Do you have the space for

a large dog? If you do not, then you should consider an adult mixed-breed dog. This way, you can be certain of his size and manageability.

There are many pros and cons to obtaining an adult dog versus a puppy. First of all, fewer adult dogs are adopted, making them more likely to be euthanized in shelters. You would truly be saving a life if you were to adopt an adult dog. Not only that, but many adult dogs are already house-trained, some are obedience trained and many are very laid-back older dogs that want nothing more than to sleep at your feet. This is less time-consuming than starting out with a puppy.

On the other hand, when you adopt an adult dog, you are also adopting his past. He might have some behavioral or health problems, but puppies can also come with this baggage, depending on their age. Ours is a "throwaway" society. What is no longer wanted

Hound mix Bella and Chihuahua mix Mario are two rescued shelter dogs that went from "pound" to "pampered" in their new homes.

is thoughtlessly thrown away. When one tires of a puppy's chewing or jumping up, the pup is thoughtlessly thrown away— dropped at a shelter, in the woods or along a roadside. This can happen to any dog, regardless of age. In the best-case scenario, the puppy or dog is traumatized by this experience but is able to overcome it in a new loving home. In the worst case, the dog is euthanized in a shelter or may be hit by a car or become sick or otherwise injured if left to roam loose. What a desperate display of irresponsibility and cruelty!

An adult dog may take longer to bond with his new family than a puppy. The strongest bonding time is between 7 and 12 weeks of age. Unless your new mixed-breed pup was dropped off at the shelter or rescue organization and adopted by you at this young age,

This sweet shepherd mix girl traveled from a shelter in North Carolina to a rescue in Massachusetts, where she quickly found a family to love her.

he will take longer to bond to you. It is rare to obtain pups of this age from a shelter or humane society unless a litter of pups or a pregnant dog is abandoned there, or a stray dam and her litter are found. The younger the dog, the less time it will take to bond with him and the easier he will be to train. An older dog may take upwards of a month to settle into a new environment, so plenty of patience is required, but the results can be so rewarding.

Older dogs are more set in their behavior patterns and will be more resistant to training. It can take twice as long for an adult dog to learn the same behavior taught in ten minutes to a puppy. Therefore, overcoming destructive chewing patterns can be easier to accomplish with a puppy than with an adult dog that has been doing it for several years. These are all considerations that you must think about when deciding whether an adopted puppy or adult is best for your life.

TEMPERAMENT AND BODY LANGUAGE
The best means of knowing what type of puppy or dog you are choosing is through temperament testing. This way, no matter what breeds are in your prospective dog's ancestry and regardless of his age, you'll be able to learn a lot about his personality and how to work with him.

This is a most important aspect of obtaining a mixed-breed dog. Temperament testing before you decide to bring the dog home will help eliminate the possibility of obtaining a dog that does not fit into your lifestyle or might clash with your personality. The results of the temperament test will give you an overall idea of how to acclimate your new dog to your home and family, and how to approach the training process once he comes home with you.

You must also realize, when you visit the shelter or rescue organization, that the dog is most likely stressed and will not behave the same in his current environment as he will after a month or so at your home. Once a dog feels at home, he has a tendency to become more territorial and demanding. The pup that once stayed by your side begins to stray, or the dog that was frightened of strangers begins to bark at them.

How you approach a dog that is in a kennel environment (such as in a shelter rather than a rescue foster home) makes all the difference. While some are jumping on the gate, others are hiding in a corner. Begin your temperament test from a short distance away. Observe the dog that you are considering for at least ten minutes. You can tell much about the dog's personality through observation. A jumping/barking

dog is one that is not at all intimidated by his environment. This might be a difficult dog to train, for he is bold and fearless. Then again, he could be craving attention very badly and, once he receives attention, will settle down by your side. However, you can be certain that this dog is not fearful, whereas the dog that is hiding in the corner is certainly a fearful dog and must be approached slowly and quietly, not forced to interact right away.

Before you can learn how to perform a temperament test properly, you need to learn about how dogs communicate. What are they saying when they bark, with their ears pricked forward and tails held high? Are they being aggressive when they pounce and jump around? When you see their teeth, are they showing that they are about to bite? There are nuances to all of these things that have very different meanings. Just because you see the dog's teeth does not mean he's ready to bite

What kind of traits are you looking for in your mixed-breed companion? Do you want a high flyer that you can train for competitive sport?

This retriever/spaniel mix looks friendly and alert with her ears up, head held high and soft facial expression.

mean that the dog is relaxed. For dogs with folded or hanging ears, look at the base.

- The ears held slightly back may mean the dog is listening or might mean a slight form of submission.
- The ears held flat to the head most definitely mean submission and/or fear. A fear biter will hold his ears flat to his head.

HEAD

- A head held high means interest or alerting to a stimulus. It can also depict a dominant personality.
- A head held at a normal angle—not high or low—means a relaxed mood.
- The head held with the eyes pointing down demonstrates submission.
- When the dog holds his head low and stretches his neck forward, this is depicting a very submissive greeting gesture, common in puppies and submissive dogs.

EYES

- The eyes say a lot. Direct eye contact is a dominant gesture. If you meet a dog that stares directly into your eyes without looking away, steer clear. This is a very dominant animal. A dog should always look away first.
- Blinking eyes are a form of submission.

you. He may be smiling, which is a very common greeting behavior in puppies and submissive dogs.

Here's a basic outline of canine communication, from their ears to their tails. Through this, you'll better understand what a dog is saying to you.

EARS

- The ears pricked forward signify alertness. The dog is zeroing in on something. The alert stance can be a form of dominance or just an interest in something.
- The ears held with their openings at the sides mean that the dog is paying attention or might even be wary of something.
- The ears held lazily at the side

- Staring, then looking away, is acceptance.
- Looking with a soft facial expression, but not directly into your eyes, means a dog who is paying attention to you. He'll blink occasionally, but not constantly. He is relaxed.

MOUTH, TEETH AND VOICE

- The mouth conveys a lot of information. Relaxed lips show a relaxed dog. Raised lips can mean one of two things: aggression or submission. It depends on how they are raised.
- A single lip between the gum and teeth, showing just the tip of the incisor, is a sign of happiness and is especially cute.
- The lips raised in front, showing the front teeth only, is a sign of submission or fear, depending on the other visual cues. This might be associated with several other forms of body language, such as the tail's wagging quickly, the head's being stretched forward and the dog's either prancing around or standing still by his person.
- If the lips are raised and showing all the teeth, way into the back of the mouth, that's an aggressive response, especially if the dog is growling in a low tone.
- The tone of vocal emission has a lot to do with the dog's expressions. A high tone, such

as a yip, is happy. A medium tone, such as a loud bark, is demanding. A low tone, such as a growl, is aggressive.

BODY

- A dog that is dominant will try to make himself look large. He'll be raised high on his toes, his head held high, his tail straight out and partly upward and the hair along his spine raised.
- A relaxed dog will remain his normal size and his tail will be held low (or in the case of a dog with a tail that curls over his back, relaxed into position). His ears may swivel from side to side, but not perk forward.
- A dog that is concentrating and/or working will have a grin on his face. Yes, it's an actual smile, often seen while a dog is

Ears pricked forward and body poised to run, this spitz/Staffordshire mix has something "chaseworthy" in his sight.

enjoying his training time. He'll prance, his tail will wag slowly and his eyes will watch with a cheerful expression.

- A dog that is inviting you to play will go down on his front end while leaving his hind end in the air, his tail wagging. Some dogs will bark, demanding your participation in the game. Many people mistake this for aggression, especially if the dog nips at the person. This is puppy play in its purest form. Your dog simply thinks you are part of his pack and need to partake in the games.

- There are two different types of submissive behavior: active and passive. An actively submissive dog is the type that might fear-bite if cornered and sees no way out. This dog will hold his body low to the ground, hackles raised, neck stretched out and teeth bared. His tail will be between his legs. Never approach a dog that shows these behaviors. Some do not growl to warn, they simply lash out. If you insist that this is the dog you want, approach very slowly, crouched down, and do not corner the dog. Take the time to allow the dog to come to you. Do not reach out to pet him. Let him sniff you first. Everything must be taken very slowly and methodically. Allow the dog to make the first moves.

- A passively submissive dog will try to make himself as small as possible. He will tuck his tail under his belly, will lower his head and might roll over onto his back, showing you his belly. Some dogs will urinate. Submissive urination should never be misconstrued as a house-training accident. He is simply showing you that you are the boss and he yields that position to you without contention.

Now that you know a bit about how dogs communicate, you will be able to perform a more accurate temperament test. There are several types of temperament tests, and the one that you use depends on your goals for your mixed-breed dog. There is a basic test that will let you know the dog's overall personality. Is he dominant or submissive? Is he fearful or relaxed? Does he accept new people and animals or not? This basic temperament test consists of seven parts:

1. Behavior observation;
2. Touch;
3. Reaction to objects;
4. Sound sensitivity;
5. Social hierarchy;
6. Social dominance and correction;
7. Reactions to other animals.

A more thorough test, called the Puppy Aptitude Test (PAT), developed by Joachim and Wendy Volhard, examines your dog's potential for specific occupations.

Are you planning on competing in obedience or agility trials? Do you want a dog who can visit nursing homes, hospitals and schools as a therapy dog? Are your goals to win the flying disk championships? The PAT test will give you a good idea of how well your dog will do things like retrieve, accept handling, accept new people and learn new things.

BASIC TEMPERAMENT TEST FOR SHELTER OR RESCUE DOGS

Every temperament test begins before you actually approach the dog. You should observe the dog from a distance for no less than ten minutes. How does the dog behave? Is he jumping around? Barking? Lying in the corner? You must read the dog outside his enclosure before entering. Before you start on the second test, you must take the dog to a quiet area, away from the noise and commotion of the kennel. You will be able to make assessments of the dog's temperament based on which of the possible reactions he has to each of the seven tests.

TEST 1: BEHAVIOR OBSERVATION

Stand outside the enclosure and watch the dog's reactions. Do not make noise, eye contact or quick movements, and do not speak to the dog. Just observe.

Possible Reactions:

1. Jumping up and barking;
2. Jumping up without barking;
3. Standing at the gate, barking;
4. Standing at the gate without barking;
5. Lying quietly;
6. Lying in a corner.

The dog that shows the first behavior, jumping up and barking, is a very bold dog. He is either very starved for attention or he wants to eat you. Only the second test, touch, will let you know for sure. Do not enter his enclosure crouched down. Keep your arms up and folded and do not meet his eyes. A direct challenge of eye contact might turn the dog aggressive.

The dog that exhibits the second behavior, jumping up, is clearly just starved for attention. Before going on to the second test, touch, be prepared to be jumped upon. Do not enter his enclosure crouched down.

Your first impression of a shelter dog's temperament comes from observing him in his pen or kennel.

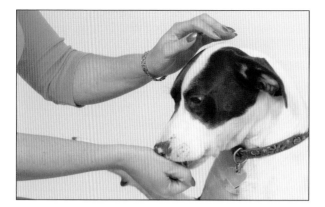

When you first meet the dog face-to-face, see how he reacts to touch. This dog sniffs the tester's hand while she rubs his head.

still be a good pet, but keep in mind that his acclimating to a new environment and becoming comfortable with exposure to new things will take some time. Should he growl at you when you enter, make sure you do not approach him at all. This is a fear-aggressive dog. While some fear-aggressive dogs eventually adjust and settle in, many can be time bombs waiting to go off.

A dog that stands by the fence with a wagging tail, whether barking or not, is surely welcoming you to play with him. This is a friendly dog that has not been traumatized by his situation. Most likely, he will quickly adapt to his new home.

A dog that lies on the floor, relaxed, may be a good candidate for adoption, but use a slow, gentle approach unless he gets up and comes to you when you enter his enclosure. If he does greet you, he will be a good candidate for adoption and most likely will quickly adapt to most any new environment.

A dog that lies in a corner is very fearful. Do not approach this dog quickly. In fact, upon entering the enclosure, crouch and do not stare. Allow the dog a chance to come to you. If he does not come, you will know that he is extremely fearful and/or traumatized. If you have the time and patience to work with him, he can

TEST 2: TOUCH
Begin by petting the dog. Rub the top of his head, his back and then his chest and tummy. Most dogs, even the overly excited ones, will calm slightly when receiving a belly rub. It is important to progress slowly while petting a fearful dog. Be patient if he moves away and allow him to approach you. If the dog does not return for attention, then it might be best to discount him from the remainder of the tests, unless you live a very quiet lifestyle without any children and few visitors.

Possible Reactions:
1. The dog growls;
2. The dog moves away, growling;
3. The dog cringes but allows you to touch him;
4. The dog allows touch, but doesn't react;
5. The dog allows touch and responds by moving closer.

Should the dog growl, you had best discount him from the remainder of the tests. He is aggressive, and you might be bitten if you do something that challenges the dog.

A dog that moves away, growling, may be aggressive and unsocialized. However, he may also learn to accept you and, if you took the time, would acclimate. Do not force yourself on this dog, for he may be fear-aggressive. Give him time to come back to you. This dog may also be ill. Dogs that have sore spots or are not feeling well may growl when surprised or petted in a sensitive area.

The dog that allows touch, but cringes, may be friendly but may have been abused at some point in his life. This dog needs your love, patience and understanding. He will work well in a quiet environment, but he could take a while to acclimate.

The dog that allows touch without reaction may be ill. Most dogs react in some manner to being touched. However, if he just lies there and accepts your touch, he may indeed do well in a home with lots of activity and new people. If you wish to adopt this dog, or any dog for that matter, your first stop should be your veterinarian to make sure that he is healthy.

The dog that moves closer to you while you touch him is starved for affection and will never get enough of it. He will most likely fit into any environ-ment, provided he receives lots of attention. This is not a dog that will do well left alone for long periods of time. Many dogs that have been tossed about from home to home experience separa-tion anxiety. They have no sense of permanent territory or family and will become destructive if their new human companions leave them alone for long periods of time.

Once the dog has accepted your touch on his upper body, move your hands down his legs, touching his paws and toenails. Many dogs are not used to having their feet touched and may react by putting their mouths on you. This is not necessarily a sign of aggression, just a lack of condi-tioning. With patience and persistence, the dog will learn to accept your touch over his entire body, a requirement for proper canine care and maintenance.

Test 3: Reaction to Objects
Take the dog to a quiet area. Make sure you have several dog toys,

Part of the touch test is handling the dog's feet.

The dog sniffs the assortment of toys.

such as a bone, squeaky toy, ball, flying disk and some chew toys. You need to assess your mixed-breed candidate's reactions to new objects and sudden noises, and his willingness to give an object back to you.

Begin by laying all the toys on the floor and letting the dog investigate them. If he easily goes to them and sniffs, he has passed the first part of the test—reaction to new things. Should he back away, it shows fear of new things. Take a few minutes, crouch by the objects and try to coax him to you. A dog that has already accepted your touch will eventually come to you and investigate the toys.

Should the dog continue to remain at a distance, try coaxing him to you with food. A piece of freeze-dried liver, hot dog or cheese might do the trick. If he still remains at a distance, then this dog may not be a good candidate for adoption unless you have

lots of patience and time as well as a very quiet household.

Should the dog pick up a toy and carry it away from you, he may easily adjust to new things but has an independent streak. This is not necessarily a bad thing. In time, and with lots of patience and training, he will learn to trust you and wish to share his toys with you.

A dog that picks up a toy and comes to you is friendly, is curious and wants your companionship. This is a good candidate for just about any home, but should not be left alone for long periods of time. He is very social.

The second part of this test is to observe the dog's reaction to moving objects. Pick up all of the toys. Using the ball or a squeaky toy, roll it across the floor.

Possible Reactions:
1. Moves away;
2. No reaction;
3. Starts to chase the object, but loses interest;
4. Chases, grabs and carries the object away from you;
5. Chases, grabs and brings the object to you.

The first reaction shows a fearful dog who should not be put in an active home. All things will need to be done slowly and gently, never forced.

A dog that does not react at all may just be very accepting of new things and noises. This dog might work out well in a noisy, active environment, provided he is completely healthy. Remember, most healthy dogs react in some way to stimuli. A dog that shows no reaction may not be completely "with it." The dog is either very traumatized or ill. Then again, some dogs really don't care what goes on around them. They're happy to just sleep at your feet.

A dog that begins to chase the object but loses interest may be curious but somewhat fearful. He may work out well in a quiet environment without children and regular visitors. Then again, he may not be into fetching. Another type of game might better suit him.

A dog that has the fourth reaction, chasing the object and carrying it away from you, is bold and may have dominant tendencies. You'll know for certain when you try the third part of this test, taking the object from him.

The dog that returns to you

with the object is a great candidate for the active home with children. He wants approval and companionship.

Part three of this test is to observe the dog's response to your taking the object away from him. This will be very important for safety if you have children at home. Give the dog a very inviting chew toy, such as a rawhide chew or beef bone.

The tester encourages the dog to return the object after having retrieved it.

Possible Reactions:

1. Growls;
2. Holds the object, but eventually gives it up;
3. Readily gives the object;
4. Drops the object and runs away.

The first reaction proves the dog to be possessive-aggressive; he could even bite someone who tries to take the object from him. This is not a good candidate for a home with children, and the behavior will need modification by working with a professional animal behaviorist. Do not

Does the dog drop the toy or willingly let the tester remove it from his mouth?

attempt to cure this problem unless you are knowledgeable about animal behavior and animal training.

The second reaction may show that the dog really, really wants the object, but will eventually give it to you if you are persistent enough. Granted, this can be dangerous if he tries to get a better hold on the object and your fingers happen to be where his mouth grips. However, if you place the dog in the sit position and, using your hand over his muzzle, press his lips into his teeth as you say "Drop" or "Give," the dog will learn to do so on command.

The dog that readily gives up the object will work out nicely in a family with children. This is a properly submissive dog that defers to your dominance without qualms or trauma.

The dog that drops the object and moves away is overly submissive. This dog will require much

coaxing and reassurance to learn how to enjoy life. He should not be in an active home with children, but rather in a quiet home with one or two adults. He may even work out well in a home with elderly people.

TEST 4: SOUND SENSITIVITY
Shake your keys, drop a book (not this one) or clap your hands. The noise must be sudden and loud to score the dog accurately. It must simulate what happens in real life when, for example, you might be walking your dog and a rattling truck passes or a car backfires, or when you drop your keys while heading for the door. Try different noises, starting with the least startling ones.

Possible Reactions:
1. Cringes and tries to hide;
2. Ignores and continues with whatever he is doing;
3. Listens, locates the source of the noise, walks toward the object and barks;
4. Listens, locates the source, but doesn't move;
5. Listens, locates the source, goes to the object and sniffs it.

A dog that cringes at the noise may be fearful of new things. He might have been traumatized in the past or just not exposed to loud noises and does not know how to handle the situation. This dog should not be taken to a home that has a lot of activity and youngsters. He would work out

Jangling keys in front of the dog is a test to gauge his reaction to noise.

best in a quiet home with one or two adults.

A dog that ignores the sound easily accepts loud noises and new situations. This dog would work out well in an active environment with children and many new experiences. However, if the dog doesn't react at all, you should also have him tested for hearing loss, as most dogs will react in some manner to the noise, even if only to look at where it came from.

The dog that approaches the source of the sound and barks at it may have dominant tendencies. This dog has become protective and should not be in a home with children and a lot of visitors unless he is responsibly trained and learns that he is not in charge.

The dog that looks toward the noise but does not move is an easygoing dog that reacts well to new things in his environment. He will easily adjust and acclimate to his new home and family.

The dog that has the fifth reaction, going toward the source of the sound and sniffing the object, is curious and well adjusted. He will work out well in an active environment with children, but should not be left alone for long periods of time, for he requires regular stimulation.

TEST 5: SOCIAL HIERARCHY

This test will tell you whether or not your candidate will give in to your demands. A dog that has the number 1 or 2 response in the social hierarchy test is a dog that will have difficulty adjusting and may be difficult to train. In many cases, you may not see the dog's true social hierarchy behavior while at the shelter or rescue group, for he does not feel territorial. The feeling of "home" may take a month or more to develop. As the dog becomes more territorial, he may also become more dominating. So, while this is an important test, it should not be the litmus test of the dog's personality. It is the results of all of the tests that count, not just one.

To perform this test, pick the dog up. If he is a large dog, just lift his front end off the ground.

In this test, the dog's front end is lifted off the ground.

Possible Reactions:
1. Struggles, growls and tries to bite or mouth;
2. Struggles, but eventually gives in;
3. Shows extreme fear and yips;
4. Gives in readily, but moves away when released;
5. Submits and returns to you when released.

The dog that shows the first reaction is a very dominant dog that would not do well in a home with children, elderly people or someone who does not intend to spend a lot of time training and involving the dog in other stimulating activities.

The dog that struggles but eventually gives in may have some dominant tendencies, but can be redirected in a positive manner and could become a good pet for an active family.

The dog that shows extreme fear will require a quiet home and lots of patience from his people. This is a fearful dog that either has had a bad experience or has not been fully socialized.

The dog that gives in readily, but moves away when released, is independent. He may not be dominant, nor is he submissive. He also won't strive to please you. This dog might work out well in an active family with children, but may prefer to live in a quieter environment. He may become more relaxed and social with obedience training and stimulating activities.

The dog that submits and returns is ideal for any environment. He strives to do the right thing and loves attention, in any form. This dog would work out very well in a family with children and lots of activity.

TEST 6: SOCIAL DOMINANCE AND CORRECTION

This test will tell you how easily your dog will learn the house rules. You must approach this test as though you are another dog. In this manner, your candidate will fully understand what you are doing and be more likely to exhibit the correct response. Dogs should never be reprimanded by shouting and hitting. Dogs do not understand these behaviors. For example, a dam's corrections to an erring puppy are quick and firm. A dog rarely actually digs his teeth in when giving a reprimand unless the opponent shows no sign of giving in.

A canine correction is done with a low growl, a show of all teeth and a quick pounce, turning the other dog over onto his back. The dominant dog will then growl and point his snout toward the other dog's throat until the other dog looks away and blinks. That is the end of it. Quick and to the point. The opponent shows submission and it is over.

This should teach you how to correct your own dog when he has done something bad. Do it the canine way. Do not overdo this exercise, however, as it can be harmful to the dog's confidence and attitude.

With this test of social dominance and correction, you will be able to observe just how easy or difficult it will be to teach your test subject. If testing a puppy, roll him over onto his back. If testing a dog over five months of age, put one hand on his collar and the other on the scruff of his neck. Do not put your face next to the dog, but do look him in the eyes.

Possible Reactions:

1. Struggles, growls and tries to bite. Comes toward you aggressively when released;
2. Struggles but eventually gives in;
3. No reaction. Remains in place even when released;
4. Gives in quickly, but cries; moves away from you when released;
5. Gives in quickly and returns to normal behavior when released.

The first reaction shows a clearly dominant dog that will give you many problems, regardless of the situation. He wants to be in control. Only a very assertive experienced owner should take him home.

The second reaction shows a dominant dog, but also one that is willing to give in to an assertive correction. He may be a bit hard-headed at times but will eventually learn the rules. Again, his human companion should be someone who is assertive.

Should the dog show no reaction at all, he is either ill or has become immune to dominant advances in some manner. Most dogs will react to this approach in some way.

The dog that gives in quickly but cries is very submissive, but may already be or may become a fearful dog. He should be treated with the utmost patience and all corrections should be very mild. He should not be in an active environment and must be watched at all times so that any bad behavior can be quickly redirected using positive motivational training.

The dog that gives in quickly and returns to normal behavior is an ideal dog. He will learn quickly and without a lot of repetition.

TEST 7: REACTION TO OTHER ANIMALS

This test is very important if you have other pets at home. You must

Rolling the dog onto his back shows how the dog feels when put in a vulnerable position.

think of how difficult it might be to acclimate an aggressive new dog to other dogs. Sometimes it is nearly impossible and your new dog has to be returned to the rescue or another home found with people who understand his situation. Being moved around only adds to his own sense of insecurity. Prevent this from happening by performing this very important test.

After your candidate has passed all of the other tests, walk him by the other kennels and observe his reactions. Stop in front of a kennel where there is an active dog (preferably one that is barking or jumping around). Sometimes a dog will not show

A dog's reaction to another dog is important. What does he do when he walks by another dog's pen?

aggression toward another dog unless provoked, and this might help you observe the dog's true reaction—before you bring him home to meet old Lucky.

Possible Reactions:
1. Goes after any dog, whether moving around or not;
2. Only goes after other aggressive dogs;
3. Doesn't show aggression, but does show an eagerness to say hello to a quiet dog;
4. Walks by without a reaction;
5. Runs by and tries to get away from the aggressive dogs;
6. Tries to get away from all dogs.

The first reaction will be very difficult to deal with in a potential pet. First of all, this tells you that you should not bring this dog home if you have other pets. There will be problems. Even if you do not have other pets, going for a walk in the neighborhood will be challenging at best. This dog will need a lot of behavior modification to learn proper social skills. Should he be over a year old, he may not ever be able to learn to play properly with other dogs.

The second reaction exhibits that the dog is dominant to other dogs and will only show aggression when challenged. The only time this can be a problem is if you are walking through the neighborhood and a loose dog comes racing toward you. It will be seen as a challenge, and your dog will try to attack it. This can also be difficult if you already have a dominant dog at home; most dogs that are already established in their territory will try to dominate a newcomer. There might be scuffles until one or the other gives in.

The third reaction, wanting to be very friendly to all dogs, is a common behavior of young dogs that have never had a bad experience with other dogs. This dog would most likely do well in a home with other animals.

The dog that walks by without a reaction is indifferent to his environment. He will most likely fit into a new home that has an established pet.

The dog that runs by and tries to get away from the aggressive dogs may instinctually avoid the more forward dogs and want to socialize with the quiet dogs because he may have had a bad experience with a dominant dog. This dog might also do well in a home with an established dog, provided the hierarchy rules are very clearly followed.

The dog that is afraid of all dogs will not work out well in a home with a very dominant dog. He should have a companion who is gentle and willing to put up with another canine who might take time to adjust. He might do well in a home with a cat or other small pet, but keep in mind that some dogs have a strong instinc-

You want a dog who is amenable to handling. How else will you cuddle with your new pet?

tive prey drive that makes them unsuitable for living with small animals. Knowing your mixed-breed's lineage will help you determine how likely he is to chase small animals.

CONSIDERING THE RESULTS

Once you complete these temperament tests, carefully consider the results. Try to close your mind to the dog's cuteness factor. This is a living, breathing, feeling being that is relying on you to give him a good and loving home. Will it work?

Think about your lifestyle. Do you have children? Are you away from home for long hours every day? Do you live in a small apartment or condominium? Does anyone in your household have allergies? Are you assertive or are

The tester claps her hands to get the dog's attention and coax him to come to her.

you a marshmallow?

You need to obtain a dog that fits into every nook and cranny, not just one that looks appealing to you. Dogs are not pieces of furniture. They need your time, energy and commitment to providing for their care.

PUPPY APTITUDE TEST
Should you be obtaining a dog for a specific purpose, such as to play fetch with or perhaps to work in search-and-rescue, you should also put your mixed-breed candidate through the Puppy Aptitude Test (PAT) to make sure he has the potential for the duties you have in mind.

The PAT should also be performed in a quiet environment, away from the other noises and distractions of the kennel or rescue location. You must have the dog's undivided attention in order to obtain valid results.

This test includes social attraction, following, restraint,

social dominance, elevation dominance, retrieving, touch sensitivity, sound sensitivity and sight sensitivity. All of these tests will give you a good idea of your candidate's aptitude for specific tasks.

TEST 1: SOCIAL ATTRACTION
Place your mixed-breed candidate in the test area. As you back a few feet away from the area entrance, try to coax him toward you. You can clap your hands, kneel down and use an inviting tone of voice.
Possible Reactions:
1. Comes readily, tail up, jumps and bites at your hands;
2. Comes readily, tail up, paws and licks at your hands;
3. Comes readily, tail up;
4. Comes readily, tail down;
5. Comes with hesitation, tail down;
6. Does not come at all.

TEST 2: FOLLOWING
Stand up and walk away from your mixed-breed candidate in a normal manner. Don't run or walk slowly. Make sure the dog sees you walk away. The purpose of this is to test the degree of following attraction. A dog that follows is a dog that will be properly social and want to work for you.
Possible Reactions:
1. Follows readily, tail up, gets underfoot, bites at your feet;
2. Follows readily, tail up, gets underfoot;

3. Follows readily, tail up;
4. Follows hesitantly, tail down;
5. Does not follow;
6. Goes in the opposite direction.

TEST 3: RESTRAINT

Crouch down and gently roll the pup onto his back, holding him with one hand for a full 30 seconds. This will test the degree of dominant or submissive tendency and how the dog accepts stress when socially/physically dominated.

Possible Reactions:

1. Struggles fiercely, flails and bites at your hands;
2. Struggles fiercely, flails;
3. Settles, struggles, settles with some eye contact;
4. Struggles, then settles;
5. No struggle;
6. No struggle, straining to avoid eye contact.

TEST 4: SOCIAL DOMINANCE

Allow your mixed-breed candidate to stand up and gently stroke him from his head to his back while you crouch beside him. Continue stroking until a recognizable behavior is established. This will test the dog's degree of accepting social dominance. The pup may try to dominate by jumping and nipping or he may be independent and walk away.

Possible Reactions:

1. Jumps, paws, bites and growls;
2. Jumps, paws;
3. Cuddles up to you and tries to lick your face;
4. Squirms, licks at your hands;
5. Rolls over and licks at your hands;
6. Goes away and remains away.

As the tester walks away from the dog, she encourages him to follow her.

Once the dog is on his back, he is held there for a few seconds. Does he relax or does he squirm and struggle to get up?

This dog is mouthing the tester's hand while on his back.

The tester cradles the dog under his chest.

TEST 5: ELEVATION DOMINANCE

Bend over and cradle the dog under his chest, with your palms up, and elevate his front end just off the ground. Hold him there for 30 seconds. This will test how much the dog accepts while in a position of no control.

Possible Reactions:

1. Struggles fiercely, bites and growls;
2. Struggles fiercely;
3. No struggle, relaxes;
4. Struggles, settles, licks at hands;
5. No struggle, licks at hands;
6. Freezes.

This dog shows interest in the crumpled paper that was thrown in front of him.

TEST 6: RETRIEVING

Retrieving is one of the most important tests for a service dog, whether the dog is intended to aid the physically challenged or locate lost persons. It is also of extreme importance for most types of competitive sports.

Crouch beside your dog and attract his attention with a crumpled-up paper ball. When he shows interest and is watching, toss the object four to six feet in front of him. If your dog is over four months of age, try throwing a ball or chew bone.

Possible Reactions:

1. Chases object and runs away;
2. Chases object, stands over it and does not return;
3. Chases object and returns with the object;
4. Chases object and returns without the object;
5. Starts to chase object, but loses interest;
6. Does not chase object.

TEST 7: TOUCH SENSITIVITY

This test is of extreme importance should you wish to take your dog into hospitals and nursing homes for therapy-dog work. Often the residents are not aware of how to properly approach and/or pet a

visiting canine. The dog must be amiable and not spook if he is touched in a sensitive area.

Take the webbing of one of the dog's front paws and press it lightly between your finger and thumb. Gently add pressure until the dog reacts by pulling away or showing discomfort.

Possible Reactions:

1. Eight to ten counts before response;
2. Six to seven counts before response;
3. Five to six counts before response;
4. Two to four counts before response;
5. One or two counts before response;
6. Immediate response.

TEST 8: SOUND SENSITIVITY

Passing this test will be very important for a therapy dog or one that will compete in performance events. Place your mixed-breed dog in the center of your testing area. Someone other than you should make a loud, sharp noise by doing something like dropping a book or keys. A large metal spoon struck sharply on a metal pan once or twice also works well.

Possible Reactions:

1. Listens, locates sound, walks toward sound and barks;
2. Listens, locates sound and barks;
3. Listens, locates sound and shows curiosity by walking toward the source of the sound;
4. Listens and locates sound but does not move toward the source;
5. Cringes, backs off and hides;
6. Ignores the sound, shows no curiosity.

TEST 9: SIGHT SENSITIVITY

This test will give you an idea of the dog's intelligent response to a strange object. Place your dog in the center of the testing area. Tie a string around a large towel or toy and jerk it across the enclosure, close to the dog.

The tester moves a toy attached to a string in front of the dog. Does he go after it or is he uninterested?

The dog interacts with another dog and the tester.

Possible Reactions:

1. Looks at the object, attacks it and bites at it;
2. Looks at the object and barks with his tail up.
3. Looks curiously and attempts to investigate or play with the object;
4. Looks, barks and tucks his tail;
5. Runs away and hides;
6. No reaction.

INTERPRETATION OF THE PAT SCORES

Mostly 1's: This dog is extremely dominant and has aggressive tendencies. He is quick to bite and is generally considered not to be a good candidate for a home with children or the elderly. When combined with a 1 or a 2 in the touch sensitivity test, he will most likely be a difficult dog to train.

This dog would not be suggested for an inexperienced handler, for it takes a competent trainer to establish leadership and positive direction.

Mostly 2's: This dog is dominant and can possibly be provoked to bite. He responds well to firm, consistent and fair handling in an adult household and is likely to be a loyal pet once he respects his human leader. This dog often has a bouncy, outgoing temperament but may be too active for a home where there are children or elderly residents.

Mostly 3's: This dog easily accepts humans as leaders. This type of dog is the best prospect for any pursuit or lifestyle. A dog scoring in this range would easily fit into a home where there are children and varied activities. In fact, he would thrive on stimulating exercises such as agility, obedience training and fetching games, making him a good performance or service dog.

Mostly 4's: This dog is submissive and will adapt to most households, but should not be forced into "scary" situations. Time and patience are key. He may be slightly less outgoing and active than the previous dog, but generally gets along well with children and trains easily. This dog might make a good therapy dog.

Mostly 5's: This dog is extremely submissive and needs special handling to build confidence. A dog within this range of scores should not be put in a home with active children, but may work out well in a quiet adult-only home or with the elderly. He will not adapt well to change and needs a very structured environment. A novice owner should not fall for his soulful eyes. This dog will require patience and the proper training approach; thus, only an experienced dog owner should take him home.

Mostly 6's: This dog is very independent. He is not affectionate and may dislike cuddling. It may be difficult to establish a relationship with him, whether as a working dog or as a pet. This is not a dog that should live with

This young mixed-breed dog certainly has an inquisitive look on his face.

children or someone who has not experienced dog ownership. He may do well in a quiet home with little commotion. This is a dog that will prefer to lie at your feet instead of going out for games of fetch.

There are several variations on the scoring that might indicate some other behaviors. For example, a dog scoring mostly 2's or 3's but that has some 1 scores in restraint is likely to bite under stress. If it is combined with some 5 scores, the independent dog is likely to hide from people or freeze when approached by a stranger. If there is no clear pattern to the scores, it is highly likely that the dog is not feeling well or is so stressed by his

It's hard to predetermine an individual's propensity for chewing, but be proactive by providing your new dog with plenty of safe chew toys to keep him happily occupied.

Coonhound/ Beagle mix Bella and her "cousin," pure-bred Italian Greyhound Django, are on the opposite ends of the hound spectrum, but they share a love of snuggling up.

current situation that you will not be able to obtain a clear picture of his "normal" behavior. In this case, you may want to try doing the test again a few days later.

SOCIALIZATION
Canines are a very social species. They prefer to spend most of their time in each other's company or with the people they love. As a new member of your family pack, your mixed-breed dog will want to always be with you. He'll feel safer touching you and, through this, the bond between you is cemented. It is a good idea to let your dog meet as many people as possible during his formative stage of two to six months of age, if you have him during this time. Take him to meet the rest of your family, your friends and your neighbors. The more people your new dog meets, the better behaved

he'll be for future encounters. This is also important for an adopted older dog.

Just as it is important for him to meet people, it is equally important for him to meet other dogs. Puppies learn many social-ization skills from other canines that people cannot effectively teach—thus the importance of exposing your pup to many differ-ent canine personalities. Most older dogs also like to socialize with others of their own species. Provided he has passed the temperament tests showing that he enjoys the company of other dogs, give him this opportunity as often as you can.

A few words of caution about doing this with a puppy, however. Puppies are very susceptible to contagions and should not be exposed to dogs outside the family until having received all necessary inoculations. Ask your vet to let you know when your pup can safely meet other dogs. Should you already have another dog who is healthy and vacci-nated, allow the two to play and sleep together. Don't worry about the pup's being too small or too boisterous for the older dog. Most dogs will tolerate many puppy transgressions and not show aggression unless the puppy is extremely obnoxious. Should there be a tussle, it normally consists only of a snarl and/or snap. This is a powerful lesson to the puppy and teaches him proper behavior. After being "taught" a lesson by another dog, your pup will respond more easily to your instructions.

Once your mixed-breed pup has had all his inoculations, you can take him to meet the neighborhood dogs at the park and participate in a puppy socialization class. If your puppy is extremely shy from the outset, you may wish to initiate the outside socialization even before he completes his vaccination regimen; ask your vet how to do this safely. Socialization classes are often offered by dog clubs, doggy day-care centers and some recreation departments. This is similar to placing young children in nursery school so that they can learn social skills and personal interactions. Taking your puppy to socialize with other puppies is a very important part of his behavior training.

Socialization is also important for older dogs. So, regardless of your mixed-breed dog's age, take the time to allow him to socialize with others of his species. This is analogous to visiting a foreign country that speaks a language other than yours. After spending a week there, not understanding the country's customs and language, how happy would you be to speak to someone from your own country? You would be even happier if that person knew the customs and

language and helped you with interpretation.

Socialization classes normally last less than an hour and meet four times. What a small time investment on your part that will pay off big! The instructor will speak with you regarding problem-behavior prevention and basic puppy kindergarten training, and allow plenty of time for the puppies to play with each other. Your pup is guaranteed to go home and sleep for hours!

When canine friends get together, they often play rough, but this is not to be confused with aggression—you will be able to tell the difference.

The two dogs interact together, using a rope toy for a game of tug-of-war.

CARING FOR YOUR DOG

There is much to take into consideration concerning the care of your new dog. He has to have the proper nutrition, grooming, veterinary care and special attention paid to specific physical conditions. He must also have exercise and proper mental stimulation. These things will allow him to be a healthy, happy dog.

NUTRITION

While nursing from his mother, your mixed-breed pup received all the nutrients he needed to remain healthy. By the age of four weeks, however, the mother dog began to wean her pups and, with the

A good dog owner truly makes her dog(s) part of the family pack.

rescuer's help, the pups learned how to eat solid food. Young puppies begin eating special puppy food that is higher in fat and protein than adult food to make sure the pups are getting the nutrition they need for energy and healthy growth.

Due to a pup's small stomach and high activity level, he should be fed three to four times per day. His metabolism acts quickly, sending the food through his system almost as fast as he eats it. Since he has small teeth, his food should be moistened with warm water or a little bit of milk. This in turn aids in his digestion of the food, for it will be partially broken down before it reaches his stomach.

Many experienced rescuers, humane societies and owners have preferences for certain food brands, having researched what works well for their own dogs. Unless your pup is having digestive problems, stick to whatever brand he was eating prior to going home with you. Should you have no idea of what he was getting, ask your veterinarian for advice and check the labels on the bags.

For most puppies, a good protein level is between 33 and 43%. The fat content should also be high, over 8%. These high levels of protein and fat are necessary for normal growth and the production of antibodies to aid in a puppy's overall ability to fight infection and heal quickly. If you've adopted an adult dog, you should also try to continue with the food he has been eating, at least initially, to avoid stomach upset. You can change to a food of your choice gradually. An adult food will not have high fat and protein levels but will provide the right balance for healthy maintenance.

A pup or adult with a super-sensitive digestive system would do well on a chicken- or lamb-based meal. Check for fillers such as plant-source ingredients and ground by-products. Corn and wheat are very common ingredi-

Providing love and attention is a huge part of your dog's proper care.

ents in commercial feeds, and many dogs have trouble digesting them. Other dogs develop allergies because of them. A premium food will not have these things included. While rice, barley and other grains as well as vegetables are good to help maintain overall vitamin balance, puppies need meat. They should get most of their protein through meat sources; these will be main ingredients in premium foods. New puppy owners are tempted to baby their new pups by offering table scraps or feeding them by hand. Don't fall into this trap. Dogs need the nutrients of dog food and need to learn to eat out of their own dishes. Be sure to feed Lucky at the same place and approximately at the same times of the day. Don't worry if he does not finish every meal. Feeding him the remainder by hand will only turn into a bad habit. Some

This Lab mix will require some attention to his feeding. First, as an active dog, he may require more nutrition; second, as a deep-chested dog, he will need bloat preventives incorporated into his daily feeding and exercise schedule.

Be careful of the plants and flowers in the areas to which your dog has access. Some are toxic to dogs, while others can cause irritations and allergies just as they would in humans.

puppies are hungrier after they've had a little exercise and therefore will eat better later in the day. Just be certain not to feed Lucky directly after vigorous exercise. This can cause digestive problems, especially if his genetics include breed(s) that have a propensity to bloat (gastric torsion, a deadly but preventable condition; ask your vet about your dog's risk and simple daily preventive measures). To be safe, always allow sufficient time for Lucky to rest before and after meals; if he's a deep-chested dog, this means at least an hour of quiet time before and after meals.

More often than not, you're obtaining a dog that is underweight. Many dogs found in shelters have been mistreated or were found wandering. Despite this, you should not free-feed him (leave his food out all day for him to pick at it whenever he chooses). This is not healthy for his digestion and can promote

fussiness. Instead, give him his food two to three times per day and monitor how much he is eating. If he is putting on weight, maintain the amount. Should he not appear to be putting any more weight on his frame, add more to his meals. If yours is a large-breed cross, do not let him get too heavy during his first year, as the additional weight puts stress on his growing frame and can lead to orthopedic problems. Using a high-calorie food might be helpful in rebuilding the body weight of a small- to medium-sized mixed-breed dog. Once he attains a healthy weight, cut back to a food that is a little lower in fat. There are plenty of maintenance diets

It is easy for any dog, particularly a dog this low to the ground, to pick items up from the ground in his mouth, something you want to watch out for and discourage.

available. Ask your veterinarian.

Puppies have a tendency to eat just about anything. While you're walking little Lucky, he'll eat mulch (which can be toxic to dogs), dirt, leaves, dropped candy wrappers and chewing gum, among other nasty things. This will often lead to gastrointestinal upset, which in turn will make him vomit or have diarrhea. It can be even worse if he ingests something even more harmful. First of all, keep a constant watch on where Lucky's little nose travels. Do not allow him to pick things up from the ground; if he does, remove the items from his mouth right away.

Should you notice gastrointestinal distress, take a stool sample to your veterinarian. A mild case of gastritis is easily treated by feeding a bland diet for a few days, such as boiled chicken or cottage cheese and rice. Once

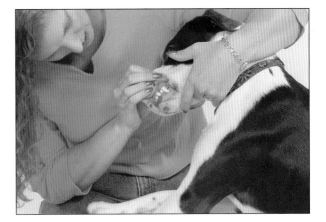

your pup is feeling better, gradually, over the course of several days, return him to his normal food. If you suspect he has ingested something harmful (antifreeze, chemicals, fertilizer, sharp objects, even toxic "people food" like chocolate, onions, nuts, grapes and raisins), contact your vet right away.

Periodically check your dog's weight. A young pup will be growing like a weed, but during his first three months should still appear roly-poly. An older dog will appear more lean through his chest and loin. Examine your mixed-breed dog by running your hand along each of his sides and feeling for his ribs. You should be barely able to feel the ribs. There should be a slight indentation at his waist and you should not be able to clearly feel or see his hip bones.

As your mixed-breed pup reaches adulthood, you can

A dog must behave well while his mouth is handled; owners must make a habit of brushing their dogs' teeth and checking their mouths for overall health.

The dog must get used to routine examination tasks such as having his ears checked.

reduce his feeding times to twice a day. If you have an adolescent dog between the ages of five and ten months, you should wean him off the puppy food and onto an adult diet. Also, vitamin supplements such as vitamins C and E will help prevent growing pains, a common occurrence in fast-growing large-breed dogs. Ask your vet about the proper age to switch to adult food and also before adding any supplements.

GROOMING

Even if your dog does not have long hair, he still needs to learn

Brushing with a grooming glove is good for short-coated dogs.

about being groomed. If you adopted your mixed breed from kennel, he will be in need of a bath right away, unless he's just been neutered (or she's been spayed), in which case, you have to wait about 10–14 days. Have you thought about how you're going to bathe your dog? Certainly not with a garden hose. And absolutely not outside if the weather is cold.

The best place to bathe Lucky for the first time would be the kitchen or laundry-room sink (if a pup or small dog) or the bathtub, if he is a larger dog. The bottom of the sink or tub should have a non-slip surface. Place a rubber mat or a towel down before filling the tub with warm water.

Have all of your supplies ready. You should have special doggie shampoo, a dry towel (or three), a toy and some treats. It may be a good idea to insert cotton balls in his ears to prevent moisture from entering the ear canal. Should you wish to do a thorough washing of his face, put some ophthalmic ointment in his eyes to prevent irritation from the shampoo.

You'll want to make Lucky's first bath a positive experience. This won't be a problem for some dogs, such as mixes with Poodle, retriever or spaniel blood. However, other dogs, no matter what you do, will still shake and pout. While he's being bathed, you should give Lucky lots of praise and a treat now and then. You can float a toy in the water, such as a squeaky rubber duck. This will make for a fun and positive experience.

Should you intend for Lucky to be a house dog, as nearly all dogs should be, then you will need to bathe him as needed to keep him from getting a doggy odor and make him more pleasant to hug. If you started bathing him in the sink as a pup, as Lucky grows you'll need to move his baths to the bathtub. He'll have more fun with the larger area anyway.

Always make sure you thoroughly dry Lucky after his bath. Never let him go outside while still damp. All dogs, especially puppies and stressed dogs, can easily catch a chill, which lowers their resistance to airborne bacteria and viruses.

Establish a brushing routine. Not only does brushing help you notice anything abnormal with his coat and skin, it also promotes

Dogs with long, thick coats need brushes, rakes or combs with long teeth to reach all the way down to the skin.

your bond with your dog. Brushing regularly removes loose hair, eliminates tangles and distributes skin oil. A longhaired dog will need brushing every day. Begin the brushing routine from day one. A shorthaired dog will require brushing only one or two times per week, but it doesn't hurt to give a quick once-over whenever Lucky comes in from time spent outdoors where he may have been exposed to insects, parasites, grasses and other debris.

The type of brush you use will depend on Lucky's coat. A regular bristle brush will work fine for a shorthaired dog, but you'll need a comb for a dog with long hair, whether it is feathering behind the legs or a complete long coat. Dogs with thick undercoats will also require a rake to get down to the skin and disengage tangles.

Begin by brushing Lucky's head and ears. Then do his chest and front legs, back, sides, tummy

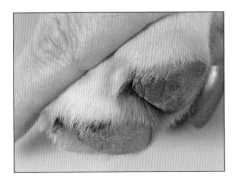

The toenails should be short and neat. You should not be able to hear the dog's nails clicking on the ground as he walks.

Different types of ears. TOP: This shepherd mix's ears are upright, meaning that he has good air circulation but also is vulnerable to debris entering the ear. BOTTOM: This retriever mix has drop ears and may have the narrow ear openings associated with retrievers.

absolutely still while this is done. At first, you might want to get someone to help you hold him while you trim his nails. This will ensure that you don't trim too closely. Cutting into the pink part (quick) of his nail will cause severe bleeding as well as make the nail-clipping experience painfully unhappy for the dog.

Look closely at the nail. It will appear similar in shape to a hawk's beak. The best place to trim is a quarter inch before the sharp curve in the nail. Above this curve will be the pulpy part of the nail, similar to the pink part of your own nail. Below this is the clear part (end) of the nail. This is the safe place to trim. Should Lucky have black nails, making it difficult to see the separation, trim off a little at a time until you are close to where the nail curves. Always file the nail with an emery board or fine file to round it off. You can also consider using a nail grinder instead of a clipper. This

Some types of liquid ear cleaner can be squirted directly into the ear. Your vet can show you how to apply ear cleaner correctly.

and hindquarters. Finish up by doing his tail. Brush gently, but firmly enough to make sure that all loose hair and dander is removed. Until Lucky is very used to being brushed, always brush only in the direction in which his hair grows.

The dog's toenails will need attention every six to eight weeks. Canine toenails can be very sharp and easily shred fabric or cut your skin. It's a good idea to get Lucky used to nail clipping as early as possible. He needs to remain

tool grinds the nail down little by little, with no threat of cutting the quick. Some dogs, however, do not like the sound of the grinder, so it takes some getting used to.

Ear cleaning is also required for Lucky's overall health, especially if your dog is the type with floppy ears. The floppy ears don't allow good air circulation to dry out excess moisture. If your mixed-breed dog is part retriever, his ear canal may be narrow, further trapping bacteria and moisture. Trapped moisture can cause an ear infection. Some infections are caused by mites and others by yeast and dirt build-up. A weekly cleaning will ensure that his ears remain healthy.

You do not want to deal with frequent ear infections, which can not only cause your dog much discomfort but also can eventually cause deafness from repeated damage to his middle ear. An ear infection is rather easy to spot. The dog will be shaking his head a lot and rubbing his ears on furniture, and you will detect an unpleasant odor in his ears. Should this occur, immediately take the dog to your veterinarian for treatment.

There are many ear-cleaning products on the market. However, you can also use mineral oil. Place a few drops on a piece of cotton. Gently clean the outer ear, taking special care around the features. To clean a little deeper,

If using a cotton swab, do so very carefully, never probing into the ear canal.

put some fluid on a cotton swab and clean very carefully, making sure that Lucky keeps still. If he is fidgety, a cotton swab could be dangerous. Do not go into the ear canal. Keep your attention on the outer ear only. Your veterinarian is the only one who should clean the dog's inner ear.

Some dogs have a lot of hair in their ears. These fine hairs can disrupt air flow, trapping dirt and moisture. Take a pair of tweezers and pull out only the hairs that come out easily. Don't pull stub-

"Look into my eyes." Mario has the large eyes typical of Chihuahuas and Chi mixes.

If you have a toy-breed mix, be aware that he may have inherited dental problems from his tiny ancestors. This is a Yorkie/Dachshund mix.

born hairs. This will make Lucky cry out and remind him of how painful the experience can be. Remember, you want to keep everything as positive as possible.

Regular eye cleaning will also be important for dogs with protruding eyes, such as Pekingese, Chihuahua and Shih Tzu mixes. Should you see

discharge or redness, this could mean either an irritation or infection. A saline optic solution can be used once a week to keep the eyes clear. Always check for dirt particles and hair in and around the eyes. In longhaired dogs, trimming the hair around the eyes will be helpful in keeping the eyes clear. Some dogs may be prone to tear-staining around the eyes; this can be cleaned with a special solution.

Something most dog owners ignore is dental hygiene. Many people think that giving their dogs hard biscuits is sufficient to scrape away tartar. This is not the case. While biscuits do help reduce tartar buildup, they do not effectively rid the teeth of plaque and tartar. The dog's gums will also need attention to prevent periodontal disease.

Even if Lucky still has his baby teeth, you should begin brushing at least twice per week. Granted, his baby teeth do fall out, but it is the process that you are acclimating him to, not just the matter of keeping his teeth clean and breath fresh.

Regular brushing will save Lucky from needing veterinary dental cleanings, which require the dog to be anesthetized, something that's always best to avoid. It will also help prolong his life in many ways. First of all, he will keep his teeth longer, which means he'll be able to properly

A doggie toothbrush or a small soft-bristled regular toothbrush can be used on your dog, with canine-formulated toothpaste.

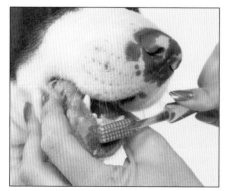

chew his food in old age. Second, it will prevent periodontal disease, an infection of the gums. Periodontal disease not only causes a dog's teeth to fall out but also transfers bacteria to his organs, reducing their efficacy and causing disease internally. While you may not see these problems while your dog is young, they will arise later, so it's a good idea to begin his home dental care early.

Toy-breed mixes tend to require more dental attention than larger dogs. Even though you may clean your dog's teeth regularly, he may still need to occasionally have his teeth professionally scaled. We've mentioned that the vet will have to anesthetize the dog so that he can gain easier access to every tooth. However, brushing regularly will decrease the number of times you have to put little Lucky through this stressful situation.

You can use a specially made doggie toothbrush, a finger brush that is specially manufactured for cleaning canine teeth or even a soft cloth. Purchase doggie toothpaste—do not use human pastes, as these are too harsh for dogs' teeth. Put some doggie toothpaste on the surface of your implement and clean each tooth in a circular motion, including the gums around the tooth. Lucky may give you the most problems in cleaning his lower teeth. Be patient and aim for one at a time. Allow him a

breather every so often. This can be especially difficult when trying to work with an adolescent dog. As many adopted mixed-breed dogs are in their adolescence, try to be patient. Take a few days to accomplish a complete dental cleaning, doing one tooth at a time. Lucky will gradually acclimate to the process and learn to accept or even look forward to it.

A pup's healthcare regimen starts with nursing, as his mother's milk provides the immunity he needs.

VETERINARY CARE

Proper veterinary care must begin as soon as you bring little Lucky home. His first inoculation should be at six weeks of age (or, if he is older than six weeks, which is

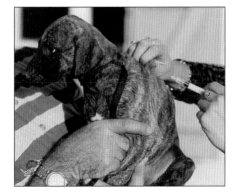

Your vet will manage all details of your dog's vaccination schedule, which is important for adopted pups and adults alike.

In the tall grass, bushes and trees can lurk nasty ticks and other pests. Be sure to discuss with your vet the best way to protect your dog, depending on the breeds in his background.

The Giardia *vaccine is an important one for all water-loving dogs and those that live in areas near water.*

likely the case, right away). This is followed by a series of boosters, the rabies vaccine and likely a kennel cough inhalant. By the time the dog is six months old, he'll have everything he needs to fight the most common canine infections. With yearly boosters, he'll maintain his immunity.

Even if you have adopted an adult dog, your first stop should be the veterinarian. While some rescue organizations see to it that all vaccinations are up to date, not all animal shelters do. Unless the dog was turned into the shelter with his medical records (very unlikely), you must begin the inoculation series immediately, before exposing the dog to other animals. You also want him to have a complete physical exam and tests for parasites.

Lucky's first three vaccines will be combination shots, called "all-in-one" vaccines. This is the

preferred method, for it involves only one shot instead of five to deliver the medication. This all-in-one inoculation includes vaccines for parvovirus, leptospirosis, hepatitis, parainfluenza and canine distemper.

Parvovirus is a disease that attacks the intestinal tract, white blood cells and heart muscles. This disease is very contagious. Young puppies are very susceptible to airborne contagions and can respond violently to parvovirus through heart failure. Left untreated, it can be fatal. Older dogs, especially those with weakened immune systems from long periods of neglect, are equally susceptible.

Leptospirosis is a bacterial disease that is transmitted through contact with either the urine of an infected dog or objects contaminated by the urine of an infected dog. This disease can result in kidney failure.

Hepatitis is a disease that attacks a dog's liver. Sometimes a

dog can get a respiratory infection as a secondary symptom. As with leptospirosis, contact with infected urine or objects touched by the urine of an infected animal transmits the disease to the unvaccinated puppy.

Parainfluenza is not as fatal as the previously described infections, but can cause much discomfort. Should your dog have contact with the nasal secretions of a dog with this virus, he can show symptoms of upper respiratory distress such as sneezing, nasal discharge and overall lethargy. Many stray dogs contract this infection due to their contact with other unprotected canines.

Canine distemper is spread not only through contact with the nasal secretions of infected dogs but also through contact with ocular secretions. This virus can also be carried on air currents or on inanimate objects. First, the affected dog would show respiratory distress and flu-like symptoms. Should he not be treated in time, distemper can be fatal. This is another infection commonly seen in dogs that have been stray for long periods of time.

There are two other vaccines that you should request. One is the Lyme-disease vaccine and the other is the coronavirus vaccine. Lyme disease is transmitted through deer-tick bites. Should you live in an area where ticks are prevalent, make sure Lucky has

Dogs that live or play together must be up to date on their vaccinations, as many serious canine diseases can be easily passed from dog to dog.

this yearly inoculation. Lyme disease creeps into your dog's system. It first causes achy muscles and lethargy. Eventually, it can cause complete paralysis and death. However, there are some types of dog, such as Collies and retriever breeds, that react poorly to this vaccine. If Lucky has any of these breeds in his background, avoid the vaccine and remain vigilant about his exposure to wooded or bushy areas. Using a topical repellent is also very helpful.

Coronavirus is usually a mild infection. However, young puppies and old dogs are very susceptible. The symptoms include diarrhea, vomiting and fever. Coronavirus is similar in many ways to parvovirus, only not as severe. Caught early, your pup will make a complete recovery. If your mixed-breed dog is either very young, old or otherwise in poor condition, request this vaccine.

There is also a vaccine for the *Giardia* bacterial infection. *Giardia* is contracted through ingesting bacteria that are often found in our waterways. A dog that enjoys swimming in lakes or rivers can easily contract this infection, causing mild to severe mucus-laden diarrhea. Antibiotics quickly cure the problem, but prevention is always the best cure.

Lucky can't tell you how he's feeling, so you'll have no sure way of knowing if he's infected with any of these problems when you get him, unless he is coming from a rescue that's seen to his veterinary needs. Make sure you cover all your bases. If his health history is unknown, get the first set of shots right away. This first set includes distemper, hepatitis, parvovirus and parainfluenza. Two weeks later, Lucky should receive his next set. This includes boosters for distemper, hepatitis, parvovirus and parainfluenza as well as his first leptospirosis inoculation. Two weeks after that, he receives boosters for all previous inoculations. The all-important rabies vaccine is given when Lucky reaches three months of age and again a year later or, in the case of a dog over four months, immediately. After the first year's booster, the rabies vaccine may not have to be repeated until three to five years later, depending on the type of vaccine used and the

laws concerning rabies vaccination where you live. All the other vaccines will need to be repeated yearly.

If you plan on attending a group training class or boarding your dog in a kennel at any time, you should request that he receive the *Bordetella* vaccine. This vaccine is usually administered in a nasal spray, applied directly into the dog's nose. The *Bordetella* vaccine guards against two strains of kennel cough, a highly contagious respiratory illness. The symptoms include coughing and nasal secretions. Without treatment, it can blossom into a worse problem, such as bronchitis.

Ask your veterinarian to also begin a parasite-control regimen. This includes heartworm prevention and flea control. There are many different products currently available to aid in this most worthy of causes. Heartworm infestation is a very serious problem and, if not caught in time, can prove fatal. You can begin the puppy on a preventive as early as eight weeks of age, although a test to confirm that he is heartworm-free is necessary first. There are several different preventives offered in chewable tablet form. Some of the new medications offer not only heartworm, hookworm and whipworm preventive but also flea control. All of this protection in one monthly chewable tablet!

Should you already be dealing with a flea infestation, or regularly take Lucky to places where he may be exposed to fleas, you'll want to use a topical solution to both repel and kill fleas. Your puppy will get a real advantage by starting with a product that contains imidacloprid. This product is applied directly onto the skin between the dog's shoulder blades. It is specially formulated to not harm a young pup's tender skin. As Lucky grows, you can switch to any number of products, some of which offer coverage against ticks as well as fleas and mosquitoes.

Another drug used in parasite-control products is selamectin, which combines both flea prevention and heartworm prevention into a topical application. It is applied between the shoulder blades and, in the case of a dog larger than 33 pounds, at the base of the tail, once per month. Selamectin will protect against fleas and many types of worm infestations; it also will repel brown dog ticks but not deer ticks, the carriers of Lyme disease. Avoid any preventives containing ivermectin if you have a herding-breed mix as some, especially Collies, have reacted very badly to this drug.

SPECIAL NEEDS OF SPECIFIC BODY TYPES

Every type of dog has its own idiosyncrasies. A few of these items were already addressed in the grooming section, such as how to care for dogs with floppy ears. You should also be aware of how

This Neapolitan Mastiff mix may be prone to the orthopedic problems of a giant heavy breed or may have skin problems due to his profuse wrinkling.

The Italian Greyhound needs some help to stay warm in the winter. Not only is this a small breed, but a very lean one, too. Consider this if your dog has this breed in his lineage.

The French Bulldog is an example of a short-faced breed; others include the Bulldog, Pug, Pekingese and more. Brachycephalic characteristics are easy to spot in mixes.

to handle specific conditions that are particular to your mixed breed's individuality, such as how to care for skin folds and allergies. Dewclaw care, anal sac maintenance and respiratory deficiencies due to a brachycephalic nose should also be mentioned.

Toy dogs are very susceptible to weather extremes and cannot be left outside when the temperatures are very hot or very cold. Their overall size makes it difficult for them to regulate their body temperatures. While outdoors in the winter, they should wear a covering, and they cannot be left outdoors during the midday heat of summer. Those breeds with protruding eyes, as some small breeds have, must have special attention paid to their eyes due to the susceptibility of foreign particles' entering.

There are several breeds that have skin folds. The Bulldog, Basset Hound, Shar Pei and Bloodhound are but a few. If your dog contains any of these breeds within his mix, his skin may tend to be dry on the outside of the folds, but moist on the inside. Particles of dirt can get inside the folds. Left alone, this can cause skin irritations. You should do a regular cleaning of all skin folds to protect against topical infections and other irritations.

Many breeds are prone to skin allergies. This is best managed by offering help from the inside out. Ask your vet about supplementing

Lucky's diet with products containing vitamin E and other amino acids, usually available in any pet store. Should you see little red pimples, blotches or loss of hair, or notice that your dog is very itchy and uncomfortable, consult with your veterinarian. He'll most likely place your dog on a special diet and perhaps offer medication to cure a possible infection.

Dewclaws are present in many breeds of dog, though most often they are removed when puppies are very young. Some large breeds of dog have large floppy dewclaws on their hind legs, and sometimes their front legs, that do not get removed. Great Pyrenees and St. Bernards are examples. If present in your mixed breed, the dewclaws will need nail maintenance on the same schedule as the other nails. An ignored dewclaw will result in the nail's curling under and possibly getting caught on something or embedded in the skin. Keep in mind that the dewclaw is actually like a finger. It does have tissue and nerve endings, making a tear very painful to the dog. Most mixed-breed dogs will still have dewclaws on all four feet.

Some dogs tend to have anal-sac problems. This is more common in small dogs, though not uncommon in any dog. The anal sacs are located on either side of the dog's anus. They

The Great Pyrenees is a large dog that can have large dewclaws, and mixes may have these traits as well.

contain fluids that are used when a dog is marking territory or exhibiting an emotion, such as fear. Normally, they empty when a dog defecates but, if impacted, they cause great discomfort. Lucky might rub his rear end on the ground or lick the area under

If you spend time with your dog and know him well, you will be in tune with his physical condition and be able to recognize when something is wrong.

Canine playmates help each other stay occupied and in shape.

his tail. An impaction can become very smelly. Expressing the sacs is even more odoriferous. The best means of ensuring healthy anal sacs is to have your veterinarian or groomer express them as needed.

There are many breeds that require special respiratory considerations. They have been bred to have shortened muzzles, which in turn reduces their ability to maintain their own temperatures through their nasal passages. These breeds include the Boxer, Bulldog, Shih Tzu, Pekingese and

Providing constructive ways for your dog to occupy himself is important for promoting good behavior and keeping him out of trouble.

Lhasa Apso. If your mixed-breed dog has a short muzzle, you must take care to never allow him to overheat. Heat exhaustion, if not treated immediately, can be fatal. On hot, humid days, it's best to keep short-faced dogs indoor in an air-conditioned room.

KEEPING YOUR MIXED-BREED DOG BUSY

Mental stimulation comes in the form of toys, games and training. Keeping Lucky busy will curb him from engaging in destructive behavior. Since you most likely obtained him from a rescue organization or animal shelter, you have no idea if he has any destructive habits like digging or chewing. In fact, he may have been turned over to the shelter or rescue because of destructive habits. However, remember that bad habits do not mean a bad dog; rather, they signify a previous owner who did not give the dog sufficient attention and training.

To prevent or correct bad behavior, offer your dog at least six different types of toys and plenty of supervision. Consider toys made of rubber, nylon, hard plastic, rawhide and cotton rope. Small dogs will enjoy squeaky and stuffed toys. Regardless of type, make sure that the toys remain in good condition; otherwise, remove them. One word of advice about rawhide: give the dog the largest possible rawhide that he can pick up and carry. Large bones are better than small ones. When his rawhide wears down or if he tears off a small chunk, throw it away. Little pieces of flat rawhide or rawhide sticks can easily lodge in the roof of a dog's mouth or his throat, causing him to choke. Also, rawhide is not digestible. If Lucky ingests a lot of rawhide, he can vomit or have diarrhea. Keep the rawhide bone as a special once-in-a-while treat.

Regardless of the toy, Lucky will be more enthusiastic about it if you play with him. In order to maintain Lucky's interest in the toys, rotate them daily. Present him with three one day and a different three the next. Each time, his reaction will be, "Oh boy! A new toy!" That's much better than his deciding that your table or chair legs might be fun to play with.

The best means of keeping Lucky stimulated is to train him and teach him tricks. Dogs love learning, especially if it involves getting special rewards and praise. Don't wait until your dog settles in. He'll settle in much faster if you begin training him right away. Puppies as young as eight weeks old are able to comprehend and respond to commands. In fact, at that age, you're essentially starting with a clean slate and a mind that soaks up input like a sponge. Waiting until later will mean

Practicing the "slalom"...as the owner walks, the dog weaves from side to side through the person's legs.

having to overcome behavioral problems and facing a resistant adolescent. Even if he is over six months of age, a new home is a great place to begin learning what is and is not allowed. Begin Lucky on the right track and he'll never let you down.

Training for agility is a fun pursuit for many dogs and owners. This dog is practicing on the weave poles.

BASIC TRAINING AND GOOD MANNERS

HOUSE-TRAINING WITH A CRATE

The foremost thing on any new dog owner's mind is how long Lucky will take to house-train. Either through past experience or hearing about the nightmares of other dog owners, you might believe this is a long and messy process. Not so. A puppy as young as eight weeks can learn to use the appropriate relief area within one week. An older dog might conquer the concept even faster. However, this does not mean you can trust him loose in the house. It only means that your pup will learn that when he is taken to a specific area, he goes potty. When he is indoors, he must still be confined and watched until he is trained and acclimated in his new home.

There are several ways to ensure house-training success: confinement, setting a schedule, praise when Lucky does the right thing, constant supervision and a trick to make things more fun.

Having a place to contain your dog will make the entire process much easier. You will need a crate or pen with an area not much larger than your dog. When selecting a crate for a puppy, you want to buy a crate that will fit him when he is fully grown. In the meantime, while he's growing, partition a section of the crate so that he does not have a mansion to sleep in. Use a crate divider to make the crate temporarily smaller. The area must be large enough to enable the pup to turn around, stand, sit and lie down comfortably. If the crate is too large, he can piddle on one side and sleep on the other without ever getting too close to his mess, thus defeating the purpose of using the crate for house-training.

Whenever you cannot spend time with Lucky, he is to be in his crate. Lucky will easily accept crate-training for it simulates a den, where a mother dog would prefer to bear and raise her young. In the wild, puppies are taught by their mothers to do their business outside their den. With these instincts already in place, your dog will learn to "hold it" while in his crate. However, there are many dogs that do have house-training problems. Their instincts were not utilized for some reason and this is usually the owners' fault. For example, a dog might have been kept for innumerable hours in a crate and was not given a chance to relieve himself elsewhere. A dog in this situation may tend to mess in his crate and not necessarily be bothered about remaining in the mess. He cannot be blamed, though, as his owner left him no other choice.

In these situations, only constant vigilance will ensure house-training success with your new dog. It'll be more difficult to house-train this type of dog, but it can still be done through proper scheduling of feeding and potty trips. You may have to take any padding out of the crate for a short period of time, for as long as there's something there to soak up the urine, the dog will continue to wet on it.

Crate-training is very easy and should never be forced. Begin teaching proper crate manners from the first day that the dog comes home. Place his toys, water bowl and blanket or crate pad in the crate. Feed him in his crate. These things will immediately give Lucky positive associations and he will quickly settle in. Allow Lucky to have access to his crate by leaving the door open during times when he's not confined in the crate. He needs a room to call his own, just in case he gets tired or nervous with his surroundings. This is especially important if you have young children. Dogs need a place to retreat when tired of playing.

Accustom the dog to spending time in his crate for one or two hours at a time. Take his water bowl out of the crate and close the door. Do not leave the water in the crate. If he doesn't drink it and then piddle (of course), he'll just knock it over and be forced to rest on a wet pillow. Should you have to leave your mixed-breed wonder by himself for long hours at a time, such as over six hours daily, do not leave him in his crate. This is not humane. It may take longer to house-train him, but there are ways to both make him feel less confined and to facilitate proper potty associations. In this situation, place Lucky's crate inside a pen, such as an exercise pen or larger chain link pen. You still don't want to give him too much space, just enough so he can stretch his legs and move around a bit. The surface should be easy to clean, such as linoleum, concrete or tile. Obtain either a small child's pool or metal tray with low sides. Place it on the side of the pen opposite his crate, water and bed. Fill the container with dirt, wood chips or sod. This will simulate the outdoors. Lucky will

To be successful with crate-training, the dog must see the crate as a happy place. Throw a toy in the crate to coax him to go in.

Scent attraction is the basis of house-training. The dog will sniff until he finds a pleasing relief site.

be most likely to do his business there. Dogs simply prefer to do their business on an absorbent surface.

Setting a schedule is one of the most important aspects of making sure Lucky learns quickly. You'll need to schedule his relief times to coincide with his feeding, play and nap times. You can be assured that most puppies will have to go potty within ten minutes after eating (this time period lengthens as the puppy matures), directly upon waking from naps and shortly after playing. A dog over six months of age has a slightly slower metabolism and therefore does not need be taken outside immediately after eating. You can wait for up to an hour before taking him to his relief area.

You should write down some observations during your mixed-breed dog's first couple of days in your home. How often does he urinate and defecate? What are his sleep and play patterns? Knowing these things will greatly aid in house-training, making it easier to take Lucky to his relief area before accidents occur. Consistency with these elements will ensure quicker success and fewer spots on the carpet. It will also make for a more

positive relationship between you and your new dog.

Here's a sample schedule for house-training a puppy:

6 a.m.: Take Lucky outside as soon as you wake up.

6:15 a.m.: Feed Lucky.

6:25 a.m.: Take Lucky outside.

After the 6:25 a.m. trip, take Lucky outside every hour to go potty. This plan will need to be continued until Lucky reaches three months of age. At this time, you can begin to "stretch" the intervals between relief times, gradually working up to four hours by the time the pup is six months of age. Many dogs can hold it for much longer than four hours, but it is not fair to make them do so. Put yourself in his place and see if you could contain yourself for 12 hours every day. Most people have to relieve themselves every four hours, so it is only fair to allow your dog the same opportunity. Should you work 12-hour days and insist that you want to have a dog, consider a dog-walking service or enrolling your pup in doggy daycare. This will allow him a chance to exercise, socialize and learn appropriate potty habits. There are dog-walkers and daycare centers sprouting up in towns and cities across the country.

12 p.m.: Feed Lucky.

12:15 p.m.: Take Lucky outside to go potty.

Continue to take Lucky outside every hour, or directly after a nap or play period.

4 p.m.: Feed Lucky.

4:15 p.m.: Take Lucky outside.

Take him outside every hour, especially if you are playing with him. Don't give Lucky any food after his 4 p.m. meal, and remove his water bowl around 8 p.m.

11 p.m.: Take Lucky outside for his last potty time of the day. Make sure Lucky relieves himself before you put him to bed in his crate. Put an ice cube (but no water) in his water dish. This will keep him hydrated through the night without making him need to urinate, plus it's a great treat.

Sometimes puppies become so distracted by the outdoors that they forget why they came out. You are standing there waiting and waiting, and all Lucky's doing is smelling the dandelions. This can become very frustrating, especially if you have to go somewhere or in bad weather. Instead of allowing Lucky to become distracted, return him to his crate and try again in half an hour. When you go out for a potty trip, Lucky needs to relieve himself immediately. Then he can be allowed to play and explore.

One of the ways to make house-training even easier is to teach Lucky to go potty on command. This will save you from waiting for him to do his business. Begin by taking him outside as soon as he wakes up in the morning. He'll most definitely have to go potty. Say a single word over and over, such as "Hurry," "Potty," "Business," etc. As soon as Lucky goes, praise him and give him a treat. Every time you take him outside, say the relief word until he performs. Always praise and make a fuss over him when he responds. Dogs become very excited when they begin connecting your words with their actions. Within a few days, your smart mixed-breed pup will be going potty on command. If you have an adult dog, follow a similar routine. The adult can hold it for longer, but initially you will want to take him out frequently to give him the opportunity to potty properly rather than be scolded for accidents. You likely won't know the extent of his house-training, so you must act as if he is not house-trained, starting from scratch to teach him the routine.

Always keep an eye on your dog while he's outside of his crate or pen. There are telltale signs of when he needs to go potty. First of all, if you always take him out the same door to his relief area, he'll most likely head in that direction. Second, should he not be in the vicinity of the door, he'll circle and sniff. Another possible cue is when he sits and stares at you. Many dogs who are grasping the house-training concept will stare at their people to get the message across. If you see any of these behaviors, you better get him outside quickly!

Should you practice these aforementioned procedures and

You can teach the dog to let you know, by ringing a bell, when he needs to go outside.

The dogs licks the food that has been put on the bell.

licks the cheese, the bell will move and make noise. As soon as you hear the bell ring, quickly take him outside to his relief area and give him his potty command. As soon as he relieves himself, give him a treat. Wow! Lucky just got double reinforcement for doing the right thing. Should you wish to remain outside and play, that's fine. This will all reinforce how pleasant life can be when Lucky maintains clean habits. In a week or so, Lucky will be going directly to the door and ringing the bell. You now not only have a house-trained dog but also one that knows how to communicate with you.

PREVENTING BAD HABITS

An ounce of prevention is worth a pound of cure, or so the old adage goes. This is especially true in the case of raising a puppy. Prevent problems from happening so that you don't have to cure them later. Sadly, most mixed-breed dogs are not obtained as very young puppies. However, the adage is still pertinent. When your new dog comes into your home, he will test his boundaries. If he learns on that first day that he is not allowed to take his meals from the garbage or make a bed of your living-room sofa, then the precedent is set and more easily accepted.

The best means of ensuring that your high-energy dynamo doesn't become destructive is to never allow it in the first place. While

still experience accidents, try teaching the dog to tell you when he needs to go outside. Since he can't stand up and say, "I've gotta go now," we need to communicate in a more universal manner. Teach Lucky to ring a bell to let you know.

Hang a large bell on the doorknob of the door that Lucky passes through to go to his relief area. The bell needs to hang low enough for him to reach it and make it move. Each time before you take him outside, rub a little cheese on the bell. Show it to Lucky. When he you may think, "Oh, he's just a puppy. He'll get over it," or "I want to give him a chance to settle in," this is not the case. Whatever you allow him to do as a pup or adult newcomer, he will also do later. As a general rule, a young puppy can't do a lot of damage, but an older dog can. For example, you allow Lucky to jump on you when he's little, but what happens when he weighs over 50 pounds? You get scratches on your legs, your silk shirt is ruined and he knocks down your grandmother! You are setting precedents in Lucky's life from the very beginning. Simply don't allow him to do something in the beginning that you don't want him to continue doing later. Your dog will not hold a grudge against you, nor will his feelings be hurt. Dogs actually become more relaxed when they understand their surroundings. Being consistent from the beginning will accomplish these goals.

Testing and hierarchical discovery go hand in hand. Puppies are born with the ability to train their people. You mere human, on the other hand, have to learn to speak canine in order to properly train your puppy. This means communicating a very basic principle: the all or none law. The dog can either *always* do something or *never* do something.

Dogs don't understand gray areas such as: "It's okay this time, but not next time." For example,

Lucky jumps on you. You allow it because you're wearing jeans at the time. But what happens when you're dressed for Sunday Mass or for an evening out? Lucky doesn't know the difference between nice and casual clothes. All he knows is that when he jumps on you, he gets attention. He learned this very quickly when he jumped on you that first time and you petted him. To keep Lucky from jumping on you when you wear nice clothes, you'll need to teach him to never jump on you at all.

Never give any attention when Lucky misbehaves, including placating him when he shows fear or aggression. This serves to rein-

A well-trained dog sits for attention.

force the bad behavior. When Lucky barks at someone, the last thing you should do is crouch down and cuddle him, saying, "It's okay honey. You'll be all right." You just reinforced the behavior!

Make the dog earn your attention and praise by doing something good, such as sitting and looking up at you for attention instead of jumping. Have him sit and wait for his food bowl; do not give him his meal when he's jumping around. Don't let him out the door until he sits first. Don't pet him unless he performs a command for you. This puts you in the top-dog position. Teaching him to do what you request before he receives anything maintains your dominance without having to be harsh in any way.

These concepts should be used for all ways that your dog can misbehave, such as raiding the garbage can, jumping on furniture and counters, chewing shoes and towels, digging in the yard and excessive barking. Saying, "Stop it, stop it," in a placating tone of voice will not solve the problem. Shouting at your dog also will not solve the problem. You must take charge and nip those problems in the bud. As soon as Lucky shows any signs of doing something wrong, such as sniffing at the garbage, digging or putting a paw on the furniture, correct him immediately by pushing him away as you growl and redirect his attention onto a toy.

CURING BAD HABITS

If your irresistible mutt has already wrapped you around his paw and begun misbehaving, there are ways to cure his bad habits in a way he understands. Lucky does not speak the human language. He speaks canine. Repeating yourself (at ever-increasing decibels) will not teach him to perform correctly or quickly and only serves to inform him that you have lost control. His instincts kick in, and, therefore, he thinks he must take over. Your mixed-breed dog knows that an alpha dog does not shout, he growls in a low, scary tone. The stance is pure threat, which in most cases is enough to rectify the situation. Dogs do not hit, yell at each other or hold grudges. Their corrections are quick, firm and to the point. The dog gives in quickly or else the threat is taken to the next level. Thus, if you shout, hit or repeat yourself to try to cure your pup of bad habits, he simply will not understand. Instead, you'll be causing worse problems, such as fear biting and submissive urination. Use canine language to make your point. Lucky will understand and learn faster, with less confusion.

JUMPING UP

This is one of the most common canine bad habits. Initially, Lucky is jumping up to say hello. When dogs greet each other, they first touch noses. He can't reach your nose, as it is way up high. He must

An example of the type of tin to use for a "no-jump" box.

jump up to give you a proper greeting. As Lucky learns that jumping up earns him attention, he begins jumping up as a means of demanding your attention. Unless you don't care about going to work or out for the evening with pawprints on your clothing (then again, you could be making a fashion statement), or you don't care that every guest to your home will be greeted by an exuberant, jumping Lucky, you should teach Lucky that jumping up is not what good dogs do.

The easiest means of teaching this is, first of all, to not give him attention when he jumps on you. You can move back as he's about to put his paws on you. Without you to land on, Lucky discovers that jumping up has no benefits, and he will stop the behavior. You have to be timely, however, for if Lucky does get his paws on you, the correction won't work.

A means of curing jumping is to make a "No Jump" box, which has many uses. A "No Jump" box is a small metal can, such as a bandage box, tea tin or coffee can with approximately 15 pennies inside. Be sure to close the lid securely.

You may want to make several "No Jump" boxes and place them strategically near doors, in the kitchen and in the family room. This way you're always prepared, and it only costs you about a buck.

When Lucky jumps up, shake the can hard in an up-and-down motion, once or twice. You won't need to do so more than this, for the noise burst will make him move away. As soon as all four feet are on the ground, make him sit. Once he's sitting, pat his head and praise him. This teaches Lucky that good things come to dogs who sit for attention.

CHEWING ON YOU

Dogs, and puppies in particular, are very orally oriented. They will put their mouths on anything, especially you. This may be cute if Lucky is a puppy with little baby teeth (although puppy teeth are *sharp*), but it will not be cute as his jaw pressure increases or if Lucky is older than five months of age. Regardless of age, this behavior may begin as exploration but turns into a form of domination. This behavior should be stopped immediately.

As soon as Lucky puts his mouth on you, take him by the scruff of the neck, look him in his eyes and growl. Continue to hold him and stare at him until he looks away first. This is very important, because if *you* look away first, you are giving in to him, regardless of

The Alpha stare lets the dog know that you mean business.

Hold the stare until the dog is the one to look away.

the fact that you are holding him by his scruff. Never look away first. Also, be aware that Lucky's blinking is an indication of his submission. You can release him after a blink or two. Holding him longer would be counterproductive.

Please note that this correction must be done quickly and firmly or it can backfire on you. Should you do this incorrectly, your dog will become more tenacious and start biting on purpose. If you are not comfortable with this procedure, try spraying a bitter deterrent or citronella on your hands just before playing with Lucky. He'll hate the taste and immediately let go of your hand. Dogs remember

whether something tasted good or bad. Why put their mouths on something unpleasant when other things, such as food-filled toys, are available? Make sure these good things are available!

CHEWING ON HOUSEHOLD ITEMS
This is a common occurrence as young dogs explore their surroundings. At first, they don't put their mouths on things to chew them, only to see if something is edible. As puppies develop and begin to teethe, their purpose changes to chewing as a form of relief for their sore gums. A rescued dog may chew because of anxiety. Unless you want to lose everything you own, including your new mixed-breed dog, start teaching your masticating mongrel which things he can and cannot chew on. Namely, he can chew on his own toys, but not on anything that is yours.

Keep in mind that many dogs are given up by their owners due to behavior problems. Destructive chewing is one of the main culprits. These dogs simply have not learned how to direct their chewing behaviors in an acceptable manner because their people never taught them. Again, not the dogs' fault! Even with an adult dog, it's not too late to teach him proper chewing habits. Separation anxiety and boredom are two other main reasons for chewing, both of which can be modified through proper training and conditioning.

There are several ways you can correct your dog, and keep in mind that there will be little need for corrections provided you are always with him when he is outside of his enclosure. One way is to use your "No Jump" box to distract him from chewing the forbidden item. Growl at him as you firmly shake the can up and down, once or twice. Then direct his attention onto his own toy by moving it around. Another means of correcting this problem is to fill a squirt gun with citronella oil mixed with water. Spritz Lucky each time he puts his mouth on the wrong item, then present a toy and praise him as soon as he puts his mouth on his own toy.

Another means of correcting this problem is to use the same procedure as when he tried chewing on you. Take him by the scruff of the neck, look him in the eyes and growl. When he shows submission, let go and turn his attention onto one of his toys by making noise with it. A squeaky stuffed toy would definitely grab his attention. Remember, you must be quick and firm with this correction for it to work.

When dogs show displeasure, their reactions are always quick and firm. As soon as the other dog submits, the correction is over and both dogs are friends again. This is the same approach you should take when training your dog. Never hold a grudge or malice toward your dog. Always direct, watch and communicate in a way Lucky understands.

TEACH THE CANINE WAY

Before you can begin any obedience training, you need to start with basic operant conditioning. Operant conditioning is a means of teaching the dog to respond to a stimulus and then receive a reward. The use of vocal tones and/or a clicking device can greatly increase your dog's learning speed. Your bright little canine will soon learn the meanings of your words through your use of specific cues.

Dogs communicate with all of their senses. They convey complex messages through their body language, vocal tones and scent glands. They show affection through touch and high vocal tones. Most dogs prefer their rewards through taste (a treat). In order for you to communicate with your dog, you must utilize a similar communication approach. We will concentrate on using vocal tones and visual cues, which are the easiest senses for us to control. Should you wish to learn how to use a clicker for training, consult a professional trainer who uses this positive motivational approach, for proper timing of the noise-making device is essential to a good outcome.

There are three distinct sounds you should use while training your

The clicker is a
small plastic
device that the
dog learns to
associate with
positive
reinforcement.

dog: a high, happy and enthusiastic tone for praise; a demanding tone for a command and a low growl tone for a reprimand. The actual words you use don't matter, provided you use the same ones for the same circumstances. Be sure to keep the words simple and easy to remember, such as "Good" with the praise tone and "No" or "Wrong" with the reprimand tone.

When giving a command, precede the command with your dog's name, such as "Lucky, Sit." This not only teaches him his name, but is also a means of grabbing his attention prior to giving a command. Say the command only one time and then make sure you back it up by showing him what to do. Never give a command that you are not ready and able to back up. What this means is that, if your puppy does not listen, you must quickly place him in the position you requested. For example, you told him to sit. He stands and looks at you indecisively with his big brown eyes. You will need to guide his little bottom down to the floor

and praise him. This teaches him the meaning of the word "sit."

Never repeat a command. This only teaches your dog that you weren't serious when you told him the first time. The more you give a command, the less Lucky will listen to you. Your voice will become background noise, like the radio playing while you are involved in another activity. The noise is there, but has no meaning. You issue the command once, then back it up. Your dog will respect and bond with you more for clarifying his understanding.

One way of ensuring that your mixed-breed dog learns the command without your having to repeat it is to first teach him the behavior without any command. Lure him into place with a treat. Do this three to five times and then add the command with the action. After several repetitions, Lucky will begin to associate the command with his action.

There are two distinct body signals that you should use while training. The first is to remain upright when giving a command or reprimand. The second is to crouch down to the dog's level when praising, playing or coaxing. In the beginning of training, there will be a lot of coaxing when you give a command, so don't confuse initially having to crouch down when asking your dog to come and sit with later training procedures. Puppies and submissive dogs require a less dominating approach and will respond better to a more attractive goal. For example, a young or submissive dog will be more likely to come to you when you are crouched down than if you are standing upright. You look more inviting and less intimidating when you are crouched down.

Eye contact is also very important. Your dog is more likely to listen to you if you look at his face. This is most important when it comes to reprimanding. Blinking and looking away from him while you say "No" will be totally ineffective. You must practice the "alpha stare," which means looking your dog in the eyes and maintaining contact until he looks away first. Always keep your eyes on him while training (this does not mean that you should stare him down the whole time!). Rather, keep an eye on him so that you're certain he does as you ask. While walking with him, however, merely peek from the corner of your left eye, for a direct stare will tend to slow him down and cause him to lag behind.

You need to work with your dog several times a day. Puppies and untrained dogs have very short attention spans, but love the stimulation, provided you offer it in short spurts several times a day. Keep your training sessions to ten minutes at a time. You never want to force Lucky to work when his attention span is lost. Short training sessions keep him looking forward to the next one.

If you are using food bait, have it prepared before you begin the training session. This means already sliced or broken up into small morsels and placed in an easy-to-access area, such as a pocket or pouch. Lucky will not stand around and wait for you as you fiddle with finding and breaking apart the treat. His mind will wander and, before you know it, he is no longer paying attention to you. The odors in the grass and insects on the sidewalk will be far more interesting.

It would also be a good idea to not be smoking, eating or drinking while working with your dog. In order for Lucky to give you his full attention, you need to do the same for him. Wait until your dog is released from his lesson before doing other things.

TEACHING TARGETING

Targeting is the first step in any training regimen. Targeting teaches your canine student to watch you. Teach him that good things come from paying attention to you instead of sniffing around the yard or piddling on your rhododendron. Regardless of the type of training, Lucky needs to first learn how to learn, and target training begins that process.

1. Hold the bait directly in front of the dog's nose. As soon as he brings his nose closer and

Targeting with a treat.

touches your hand, praise him (if using a clicker, click it) and give him the treat. The praise (and click) acts as a bridge between your command and the advent of giving the dog his treat. Thus, he will learn to look forward to your praise as much as the food or toy reward. If using a clicker, click it as you say "Good," and give the treat.

2. This time, place the bait in your hand and let Lucky touch his nose to your hand. Praise him, but don't give the treat. First move your hand a little to the left. When his nose follows your hand, praise him and move your hand a little to the right. As soon as his nose again moves with

your hand, praise (and click) and give him his reward. He is now targeting on your hand.

A dog that shows no response to any type of reward will be far more difficult to train and may not respond easily to this approach. A different type of training procedure will be necessary. However, you may want to try either waiting until he is very hungry, such as at mealtime, or offering a different selection of rewards. There are very few dogs that will not respond to some type of food or toy.

There are a few general rules you'll need to consider before commencing any training regimen, including targeting, which is the start of training. First of all, make sure that your mixed-breed dog is well rested. A tired dog has no stamina and will not be able to work for very long. Secondly, make sure that he is not full. It's not a good idea to train him after he eats. In fact, just before mealtime is a terrific time to train. He is hungry and eager to earn his dinner. Third, make sure that you begin all training in a fenced area with no distractions (noise or otherwise). This will ensure the safety and security of your dog as well as afford you his complete attention.

THINK POSITIVE
Everything you do with your dog should be positive. Training is no different. Should you want your attentive mutt to do what you ask

and look forward to working for you, he must have fun while he is performing. That is where play-training comes in.

Lucky thinks he's playing, when in actuality he is learning. It's the same concept as offering educational toys to children. This type of training is the most positive means of obtaining fast results that last a lifetime. A dog having fun will maintain a longer attention span and look forward to each training session. Older dogs also benefit from this approach. Many mixed-breed dogs have a past that may have included neglect or abuse. Coaxing a rescue dog to learn will teach him to trust and love you more so than forcing him. This is not to say, however, that some dogs do not benefit from a more assertive approach. Some do require this in order to begin learning that they are not in charge. However, a positive approach should be the first method tried. After doing a temperament test, you should have a good idea of which approach will be most successful.

Begin each training session by having the dog target. This gets his attention and prepares him for learning new behaviors. In fact, he'll easily learn how to sit within the first two minutes of the targeting exercise. Many dogs that have dominant tendencies will still respond well to initial target training. It is only when working with specific behaviors, such as heeling around distractions and performing a down on command, that the handler might need to utilize a more assertive approach.

BASIC COMMANDS

TARGET AND SIT

Begin this first training session by giving the dog a treat and saying "Good" as he takes it from you. If using a clicker, click before giving a treat. Do this several times. Next, hold the treat in your fingers, place your hand within his reach and wait for him to touch your hand with his nose. Say "Good dog!" and give him the treat. Repeat this two or three times.

Next, move your hand a little to

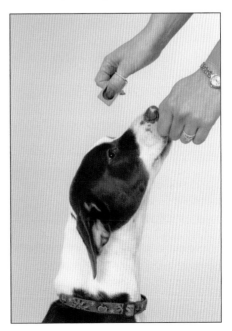

Targeting with a clicker, clicking and then giving the treat.

Holding the targeting hand (with food) between the dog's eyes.

important, for your dog can't learn if you do not first obtain his interest. Lucky will learn the target and sit exercise within a few minutes.

COME AND SIT

One of the most important things your dog can ever do for you is to come to you. This is one of the easiest behaviors to teach a puppy. Puppies are very insecure until they reach the age of about five months. He'll want to be near you at all times. An older dog may not be as willing to respond and should be leashed so that you can back up your recall (come) command by pulling him to you, if needed. This is especially true of a

Giving the dog the treat after he sits.

the left and then the right. As Lucky keeps his nose on target, praise him and give him his treat. Add an up-and-down motion. Each time Lucky follows the target, reward him.

Now we'll teach him to sit. Place your targeting hand in front of his nose and lift it slightly upward toward his eyes. As you do this, say "Lucky, sit." Your dog will be watching his target and, as his head moves upward, his rear end will go down, like a see-saw. The moment his rear end touches the ground, praise him and give him his reward. Through this exercise, you are teaching Lucky to stop whatever he is doing, remain still and pay attention. This is very

dog you have obtained from a shelter or a rescue organization. Many have learned to ignore people and not rely on them for comfort. The bonding will take time and patience. Be certain you have a means of backing up your command with a dog that might be indifferent to your presence.

Put your targeting hand under the dog's nose. Let him smell the treat and then step backward two to three steps as you say, "Lucky, come," in a happy tone of voice. He'll immediately follow his target. Praise him enthusiastically as he comes toward you. If using a clicker, click at the moment he looks at you and give him a treat. Then make him take a few steps toward you, click and give the treat. Build on his positive behavior in gradual increments. Don't expect the finished product right away.

When you stop moving backward, bring your hand over his head to an area just between his eyes so that he must look upward. Be sure your hand is not more than two inches from his nose or he'll likely jump up. While he's looking up say, "Lucky, sit." As soon as his rear end goes down, praise him and give him his treat.

Continually increase your number of steps backward as you practice the come command. This way, Lucky will learn to come from increasingly longer distances. Always make him sit when he

arrives. The last thing you want Lucky to learn is to come and then leave, or to come and jump up. A come and sit maintains his attention on you and teaches him appropriate behavior patterns.

Once the pup is reliably responding to the come and sit commands, this is the opportune time to get him accustomed to a leash. Attach a lightweight nylon or cotton leash (anywhere from 4 to 6 feet in length) to his regular neck collar. Let Lucky drag the leash while you work with him. This will allow him to acclimate to the feel of the leash without having it pulled on or used in a manner that he does not understand.

Begin teaching the come exercise by holding your food hand under the dog's nose.

Start to move backward as the dog targets on your hand, thus moving forward toward you.

Targeting in the heel position.

ROUND ROBIN

Now that Lucky has learned to obey "Come" and "Sit," it's time to involve the entire family. First of all, everyone must do the come and sit exercises with him individually so that he learns to listen to everyone. Then two of you stand about 6 feet apart, facing each other. These are the positions for the Round Robin game. The Round Robin game is the fundamental means of teaching the dog how to perform specific behaviors such as sit, stay, down and come. It is also a positive means of teaching older dogs that might be a bit shy or unsure of their environment. Through play-training in this manner, the dog learns that everyone has only the best intentions toward him.

This type of training also has many benefits. First of all, Lucky has a great time, thus maintaining a longer attention span. Secondly, he learns to work for everyone in the family, not just one person. Third, he will become very tired, needing several hours of rest afterward. A tired dog stays out of trouble, thus giving you peace of mind for a period of time.

Begin by calling the dog to come. As soon as he sits and receives his treat, the next person calls him. The dog will come to each of you in turn and sit facing you. Go back and forth a few times, then increase the distance between you by taking one big step backward while the other person has the dog's attention. You can continue increasing the distance up to about 15 feet. More than that would be too much at first.

Should Lucky become distracted during his travels between family members, the person who last called him should try to regain his attention by putting a treat under his nose. If this is not enough, then that person should take hold of the leash and bring the dog to him. This is very important, for Lucky will quickly figure out whose voice has meaning and whose does not. Dogs will not listen to those who do not back up their commands.

HEEL AND SIT

The Round Robin and come and sit exercises will easily be transferred into heel and sit work. Lucky already knows most of it. He knows to follow the target and that when he arrives at that target, he must sit to receive it. Thus, all you have to do is transfer your target to your left side instead of holding it in front of yourself. The dog will then go to your left side and sit.

Begin by having your smart mixed breed do a come and sit. As soon as he sits, place yourself at his right side, your leg even with his shoulder. This is the proper heeling position. It is important that Lucky learns to remain in this position; otherwise, he cannot be properly attentive.

Once at his side, maintain his attention by keeping your target on your left leg at knee level. When his nose targets on your hand, offer the reward as you praise him. Once he's finished with his treat, say "Lucky, heel" and take a step forward on your left leg. Moving your left leg first becomes Lucky's visual cue for the heel command. He'll learn to move forward as your leg moves forward.

Go only one step and stop. Lucky will most likely follow his target and move forward with you. As soon as he does, praise him. When you stop, say "Lucky, sit." As soon as he sits, give him the treat. Keep increasing the number of steps you take each time you do the heel exercise. Within a short time, you and Lucky will be walking 5, 10, 20 steps and more. Once

you get this far, you can begin incorporating turns. Do a turn and stop directly after the turn. This will keep the dog at your side. During later training, executing turns will be the best means of maintaining his attention.

If, at any time, Lucky becomes disenchanted by his target and more interested in a leaf blowing by, place the reward under his nose and draw him closer to you. Decrease the amount of steps between your start and stop. Maybe his current reward is not inviting enough. Try something else. If he was interested in that stick, maybe holding it would maintain his attention. The reward does not always have to be food.

Another thing you can do to maintain his interest once he's

Walking in the heel position while targeting.

Maintain the hand signal for "down" (finger pointing downward with treat held between thumb and finger) while you move your hand toward the floor. The dog's head will dip down to follow the treat.

gotten pretty good at heeling is to alter your pace now and then. Lucky must learn to remain at your side whether you are walking slow or fast. In fact, one of the ways to obtain the attention of a distracted dog is to jog a bit. Most dogs will eagerly run after a fast-moving playmate. Just don't let him think you're a playmate, for your dog must always know that you're the pack alpha. Change the pace in short bursts. Always praise Lucky as he catches up with you. Should he overshoot, turn to the right and lure him back to your side.

Once your hand reaches the floor, the dog may fully assume the down position or may need some gentle pressure on his shoulders.

DOWN

The next command on your training agenda is the down. This is initially taught during the Round Robin game. It should be interspersed with the sit command. For example, on one round, Lucky sits; on the next round, Lucky sits and then downs before the next person calls him.

The down exercise can sometimes be difficult to teach because it is a submissive position. Should Lucky have a dominant personality, or derive from breeds that are traditionally guard dogs, he will not easily accept the down command. However, this is even more reason to begin teaching him this behavior as early as you can. While your puppy is young or your dog is new to his environment, he is less likely to test his pack position than when he reaches the more independent age of 18 to 20 weeks or has lived in your home for over 2 weeks.

Targeting is the easiest means of teaching the dog to lie down on his own. Place the treat between your thumb and middle finger. When Lucky arrives and sits, let him smell the treat as you point down at the ground between his front toes. His head will dip downward. Most dogs will follow their heads and bring the rest of their bodies down as well. Should your individual not do so on his own, apply gentle pressure on his shoulder blades. He should easily drop on his belly. As soon as he has completed the criterion for this command (meaning he is in the down position), give him lots of praise and his treat.

Be absolutely certain to vary your request for the down, meaning that you should not give the down command after every come and sit. This is very important, for you don't want Lucky to believe that he always arrives and lies down. He should always come in and sit first, and await his next command.

Dogs are easily pattern-trained. Should you repeat something as few as three times, Lucky will learn the pattern and tend to anticipate your commands. While it's nice to know that your loving mutt really wants to please you that much, it does not mean that he's obedience-trained, only pattern-trained.

STAY

The next command your mixed-breed superstar will learn is the stay. This can be the most difficult thing for a puppy to learn. Young dogs are constantly in motion. Remaining still in the same spot is not on the top of their agendas. However, dogs over the age of seven months generally have no problem with this command unless they are very insecure or hyperactive.

The stay command will need to be done through a gradual increase of your criterion, using a method called successive approximation. This type of training is used when-ever gradually increasing the criterion for any given exercise. For example, when you began teaching Lucky to heel by taking one step and building on that, you used successive approximation. As he accomplished two steps, you went on to more steps in between each stop and sit. Before long, you were walking ten steps and doing turns. You successively increased the criteria that Lucky needed to demonstrate in order to earn his reward.

Begin teaching the stay exercise by first playing the Round Robin game. When Lucky arrives and sits, place the palm of your hand in front of his nose (not touching him) and say "Lucky, stay." Hold the treat near his nose but don't give it to him for three to five seconds. Praise him as he remains in place. Give him his treat

The dog stays during the Round Robin game.

Moving around the dog in the stay.

Gaining distance in the stay.

"Good boy." The first time you do a stay, you'll say "Good boy," one to two times. The next time, he stays for two to three "Good boys." And so on, until Lucky can remain in place for at least 30 seconds.

By the time you reach five to six words of praise, Lucky may start popping up and trying to go to the next person, who might be more willing to offer a treat for a simple sit. You can prevent this by stepping on his leash when he arrives and sits before you. Should he get up, you can easily bring him back into position and repeat your stay command. After replacing him in approximately the same location, again tell him "Stay," but this time shorten the amount of time to two or three "Good boys." Sometimes you need to regress in order to progress. When working with a

and then the next person should call him to come. Each time you have Lucky come and sit, increase the amount of time that he has to maintain the stay position before receiving his reward.

Since you'll have a lot to do within a short timeframe, looking at your watch to count how long he stays is not something you can coordinate. You can more easily count the seconds by using "Good boys." One second equals one

Progress the same way as with the sit/stay to teach the down/stay, starting out very close to the dog.

puppy or a dog that has a past of neglect or abuse, everything needs to remain as positive as possible. Going back to a comfortable zone in which he performs successfully (in this case, less time in the stay) increases his desire to please you.

Each time you have a training session, increase your pup's stay time. In a few weeks, he'll be able to remain in one spot without any problem. Practice the stay exercise with the down position as well. Remember to vary all of the exercises in order to keep Lucky attentive.

When Lucky is able to remain in the sit/stay for more than 30 seconds, it is time to introduce the next variable—your moving around him as he remains sitting. This needs to be done with a gradual increase of movement. You begin by stepping from side to side while you stand in front of the dog, facing him. Then, the next time you do a stay command, you walk back to front along either side of him— from head to back legs on both sides. When Lucky remains sitting throughout your movements, you can begin doing a complete circle around him.

Always replace your puppy into position every time he gets up. He must be replaced as close as possible to the original location where you told him to perform his sit/stay. This way, he learns to remain where *you* told him to stay, not where *he* chooses to stay. Even being allowed to scoot into a new position following your movements will decrease the possibility of Lucky's learning to stay in one place. He must remain where you put him, facing in the same direction. His head can follow your movements, just not his body.

As Lucky accepts your walking around him, try doing so in both directions. Then, begin to increase your distance away from him as you move around him. Add a foot or two of space between you and Lucky each time you do a sit/stay. Within several training sessions, you should be able to get six feet away from him as he remains in his sit/stay.

Practice these movements with the down/stay as well. The only difference will be that instead of your stepping in front of the dog, you'll start with side-to-side movements along his right side and proceed to walk around him by going around his back end first. This way, Lucky is less likely to get up.

WORKING WITH A TRAINER

Often, a mixed-breed dog is given up due to behavioral problems that stem from the dog's not having been properly obedience-trained while still a puppy. When distracted, a dog like this may not respond to food or toy rewards and will continue to misbehave despite your placing the bait directly under his nose. This is a situation in which you should obtain the services of a professional animal trainer and/or behaviorist.

Finding a good trainer for your dog is as important as finding the right therapist or medical doctor for yourself. A professional trainer will be able to quickly figure out the proper training approach for your pooch and apply the training procedures in a positive manner, regardless of your dog's problems. For example, should your dog have a problem with aggression toward other dogs, the last thing a trainer should advocate is hitting, yelling or dragging the dog around by his neck. Dogs do not understand these behaviors and will become worse when confronted with them. All training should be done in a manner that your dog will quickly understand and enjoy.

When searching for a trainer, check with your veterinarian, your groomer, a local doggy daycare center and other dog owners whose opinions you trust. The best trainers are those to whom people will refer others. Generally, the referral comes from someone who has had a good experience with the trainer. There might even be a regular working relationship between animal professionals, which is always a positive sign; for example, a trainer who works in conjunction with your veterinarian.

There are three basic ways that trainers operate. The first is by offering a low-cost group class. The group usually consists of four or more dogs and their owners and is given at a specific place and time for a series of four to ten sessions, depending on the trainer's goals for the class. In this situation, it is difficult for the trainer to address specific behavioral problems in individual dogs, as he wants to keep the entire group advancing. Should the class have more than ten dogs, it is unlikely that you will get anything out of the sessions and your experience may be frustrating. There are some very good trainers that offer instruction in a group setting, but you will have to choose carefully and your best bet is to get a trusted referral. If you are planning on signing up with a group class through a pet-supply store, find out about the trainer's credentials. Depending on the trainer and the store that sponsors these classes, the trainer may or may not have the option of approaching each dog and owner as individuals and thus may or may not be a viable option for you and Lucky.

The second means of training is to send your dog away for anywhere from two weeks to over a month. This is the most expensive means of accomplishing your goal of a trained dog, and you also will have very little input in the training process. It works fine as a jump-start into the training process if you must be away for a period of time and don't wish for your dog to languish in a kennel. Sending him off for training will give him more stimulation and exercise while you are gone. However, unless you have done extensive research on the trainer and the facility (i.e., visited the facility and watched the training sessions and methods used), the chances of your dog's not being treated the way you want are very great. Be certain to do your homework and speak to others who have used this service. Investigate the areas where the dogs are housed. Should Lucky be kept in a large kennel, where many other dogs are also being housed for training, you can bet that he will receive only minimal attention and not much in the way of socialization. If the trainer accepts only a limited number of dogs, say one to four, then you can be fairly certain that your dog will receive more attention and socialization, especially if

Different dogs respond to different types of training. Even in a group training class, the instructor should give each dog individual attention.

the trainer keeps the dogs in his own living quarters. When the training process is complete, you should receive complete instruction on how to work with your dog from that point on. This may include attending additional training sessions with your dog, depending on the situation.

The third means of training your dog with the help of a professional is to partake in individual sessions. This one-on-one situation allows your trainer to get to know you and your dog, address your particular concerns and give you the best advice and help on solving your dog's behavioral problems. Some trainers will even come to your home, giving them the fullest insight into the situation. The training is geared toward the personalities of your pet and yourself. You are taught how to train your dog and handle difficult situations as they arise. This service will cost a little more than a group class, but you will be getting the most for your money with this type of training. However, for this to work, you must practice with your dog as suggested by your trainer and maintain the training through daily practice sessions at home even after your meetings with the trainer have ended.

How can you differentiate between a good trainer and one who is mediocre? First of all, a professional trainer may be a member of a professional trainer's association, such as the International Association of Canine Professionals (IACP), the Association of Pet Dog Trainers, (APDT) or the Society of North American Dog Trainers (NADT). Members of these organizations usually strive to stay current with training methods and issues.

It will also help to ask the right questions when you phone a trainer. The following are a sampling of questions (and answers) that will help you find the right trainer for you:

• How many years have you been a professional trainer?

Professional trainer means that this is the person's prime means of earning a living, not a part-time job. A person who has worked in the field for five or more years is someone who is dedicated to his career and has received appropriate experience in the field. However, someone who has been training for over ten years is even better. The longer the person has been training dogs, the more experience and knowledge he has acquired. However, it can also mean that the person might be using old methods involving force or pain-induced response. Thus, the next question.

• What are your training methods?

A trainer should be able to describe his basic beliefs and methods and even offer you a chance to observe a training class in progress. There are many ways to train a dog. A professional trainer will not adhere to just one method, but will be open to trying different approaches to ensure success with your dog. Every dog is different and therefore every trainer needs to be open to using what works, provided it is done humanely and without harming your dog in any manner. A one-method trainer is one who is not experienced enough to work with every problem that might be encountered.

• How would this trainer approach the particular problems you are experiencing with your dog?

Even though the trainer has not met your dog, he should be able to give you some idea of how the training will be performed based on the information you give him.

• Does this trainer have experience with destructive or aggressive dogs?

This is very important, for if the trainer uses only one training method, it will not work with all dogs. This trainer may not work with dogs that exhibit behavioral problems. It is best to clarify this issue before meeting with the trainer.

• Is this person willing to teach you how to work with your dog?

A good trainer spends most of the session teaching you how to communicate with and work with your dog. Teaching the dog is only part of the service. The dog is bound to perform well for the trainer. Reality dictates, however, that the dog must perform well for

Tandem training with head halters. Find out which types of training methods a trainer uses before you enroll with her.

you. This person must be proficient at instructing people as well as teaching dogs.

• Will all of your concerns be addressed in this trainer's class?

Sometimes a group class is not the best approach when dealing with behavior-modification issues. A group class covers basic behaviors. Working with the trainer on an individual basis will offer more opportunity for the trainer to address all of your specific concerns. If opting for a group class, make certain that the trainer makes time for individual owners, dogs and issues unless you are simply searching for basic training knowledge.

• Has the trainer published or produced anything pertaining to dog training, such as a book, article, pamphlet, etc.?

A trainer who takes the time to

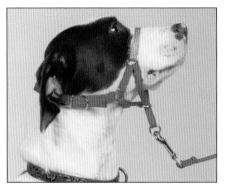

The "comfort trainer" head halter.

The "snoot loop" head halter.

read and write about training is someone who is serious about his work and wishes to provide the best service he can. Many professional dog trainers wish to share their proven methods and abilities through various modes of communication. In addition to books or articles, handouts and other written material help students learn and offer a means of help when the trainer is not available. Also, it is difficult to take notes while participating in a training class. Having the pertinent information already written is helpful for future reference.

Should you not have access to someone who can offer a positive referral to a trainer, search the Internet and find members of the International Association of Canine Professionals (www.dogpro.com), the Association of Pet Dog Trainers (www.apdt.com), the Society of North American Dog Trainers (www.inch.com/~dogs/profile.html) or the American Dog Trainers Network (www.inch.com/~dogs). All of these sites offer long lists of trainers and you can look for those in your area. Membership in an organization does not assure that a particular trainer is right for you, but is a good starting point. You must still do your research. Other informative sites are www.K9trainers.com and the American Kennel Club website (www.akc.org).

TRAINING WITH A HEAD HALTER
If you own a troublesome dog, you may wish to learn to train with a head halter. Head halters come in a variety of styles, but should never be used unless you are working with a trainer who is knowledgeable about their proper usage. As with any training device, the dog can be injured by the head halter if it is not used properly. While a choke chain can cause scarring around the neck or tracheal damage, or a prong collar can cause puncture wounds, the head halter can cause subluxation in the cervical spine, requiring your dog to receive chiropractic care. All train-

ing devices must be used properly for the optimum results without causing harm to the dog. If you are uneasy about using a training device, you can still train your dog effectively with clicker or lure and reward training.

If you and your trainer decide to try a head halter with Lucky, the communication techniques remain the same regardless of the training device: various vocal tones and visual cues, consistency and training maintenance. The main difference is that you'll be using a tool that will emulate a mother dog's correction to a puppy—pressure on the muzzle, coupled with a growl. In order to apply the appropriate pressure, you must pull downward on the leash. An upward pull, such as one used with a choke, prong or flat collar, would only force the dog into a sit.

Head-halter training is a most useful tool to use on dogs that pull hard, show aggressive or dominant tendencies or have behavioral problems. About 80% of problem dogs benefit from this tool; the other 20% do not acclimate to wearing a head halter or are simply not in need of one. Should the dog be boisterous, dominant or just ignorant of appropriate behavior, the correct use of a head halter will expedite the training process without causing physical or emotional harm to the dog. In fact, many trainers who advocate purely positive training methods will choose to use

a head halter on a pulling or disobedient dog in preference to any other training tool.

There are several types of head halters on the market. Of these types, there are two configurations: the conventional head halter, which appears much like that of a horse's halter, and the figure-8 head halter, which consists of two straps (one over the nose, the other behind the dog's ears).

There are currently a few popular brands on the market, all of which can be found at a well-stocked pet-supply store. The type of head halter depends on the build of your dog. A dog that has a short,

The "gentle leader" head halter.

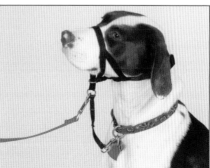

The "halti" head halter.

Moving forward into the heel, using the head halter.

broad muzzle should use a conventional head halter with a very narrow, soft strap over the nose. A dog with little space between his forehead and eyes should also wear a head halter with a soft, narrow nose strap. Due to the clamp beneath the chin, the figure-8 head halter is one of the few that will stay in place regardless of the dog's fidgeting or fussing, but is normally not the most comfortable. This type of head halter is supposed to be worn with a snug fit both behind the ears and over the muzzle. If you have an aggressive dog, you might prefer to have something that remains on the dog at all times. The

The proper heel position with the head halter.

other head halters should only be worn by the dog while you are working with him, for there are many ways that dogs can pull them off their noses and either chew them to pieces or slip out of them should the back strap loosen. You should always keep the dog within sight and busy with an activity while he is wearing a head halter.

The following explanations detail how to use a head halter to teach a few basic exercises and to correct problems. Again, though, you should not attempt head-halter training without first obtaining instruction and guidance from a qualified trainer.

HEEL AND SIT
Another advantage of the head halter is that far less effort is

needed to ensure that your dog pays attention to you. Head halters reduce a dog's pull by up to 90%. Maintain a loose leash, keeping it on the right side of your dog's head. Hold the leash in your right hand (if using food or a toy as bait) and put the bait in your left hand. If you are not using bait, as a few dogs do not care about it, hold the leash in both hands. Your left hand should be palm downward, within 3 feet of Lucky's head-halter ring, no closer. Hold the remainder of the leash in your right hand. Keep both arms down and close to your body.

Regardless of the tool you use, teach the heel and sit in small increments. This is not only to acclimate the dog to the head halter but also to teach the dog the meanings of heel and sit instead of merely forcing him to follow you.

Turning left while heeling.

Begin in a similar fashion to the lure and reward method, with taking just a few steps forward and coaxing the dog to catch up, then giving the sit command and placing the dog into position if he has not already done so. In this manner, you are showing the dog the meaning of each command by coaxing and placing him into position. After several repetitions, it should begin to make sense to him.

When he is readily remaining with you as you take up to five steps forward, gradually increase the amount of steps. Then, add turns and changes of pace. The more you vary the movements, the

Turning right while heeling.

A sharp 180-degree turn when the dog plants his rear.

more the dog will remain attentive to you.

When correcting for forging ahead, use a smooth downward pressure and pull in the direction opposite to where the dog's head is faced. For example, your dog is looking to the left at another dog. Prior to his ripping your arm from the shoulder socket, pull downward and turn to the right. His attention will be returned to you just as he was thinking about going to greet the other dog. Waiting until he has already left your side will require you to utilize more muscle and employ more careful procedures to ensure you don't yank on your dog's neck, so it's better to nip his lack of attention in the bud. Timing is everything.

Should Lucky go behind you and up to your right side, do a left turn. This need not be done with any leash pulling. Simply turn 180° to the left. Lucky will automatically end up on your left side.

Some dogs will balk at moving forward. There are several ways to

Crouching down to coax the dog to catch up.

overcome this "planting of the behind." One is to do a sharp 180° turn down the dog's right side. This will both turn him in the opposite direction and bring him to his feet. Another is to crouch down to his level and appear less intimidating. You also could offer a treat or toy. If none of these works, you will have to make the dog listen by pulling the leash down and forward. Don't drag him. Pull and release, offering him a chance to gain his own momentum. With the pressure of the head halter behind his ears, he will move forward. As soon as he begins his forward movement, release the leash and coax him to catch up by slapping your left leg and using an enthusiastic tone of voice.

Throughout the initial week of working with a head halter, be certain to stop and have him sit

very often. Failing to do so will result in his losing his attentiveness and your having to correct him more often. In summary, the most efficient and humane means of correcting inattentive heeling is a downward pull in the direction opposite the dog's intent to forge.

OTHER COMMANDS

The other training procedures for stay, down and come are very much the same as with lure and reward or click and treat. The only difference is that instead of jerking when the dog does not listen, you employ a smooth pull that will create pressure on the dog's muzzle, thus communicating to him that he is incorrect.

We've mentioned that the down command, in particular, may

Sit/stay with head halter.

be difficult to teach a dog that has dominant tendencies since the down is a submissive position. You will need to employ much patience and persistence to ensure that your

Down/stay with head halter.

When the dog is off leash, correction for jumping up is to step backwards, away from the dog, so that he cannot get his paws on you.

dog learns that this is just another exercise, not a harsh punishment. When teaching the down/stay with a head halter, there is no means of enforcing the command other than placing the dog into the down position. However, should he try to mouth your hands and arms as you place him, you can pull down and forward on the leash with your right hand as you apply pressure to his shoulder blades with your left, along with unbalancing him by pressing him away from you as you place him down.

Head-halter correction for a dog that mouths and does not go down on command.

BEHAVIOR MODIFICATION

Very few adopted mixed-breed dogs come with a clean slate unless they are very young puppies with-out past issues. The head halter will aid in your efforts to overcome problems such as aggressive tendencies toward other dogs, the need to play with every dog in sight, excessive barking and jumping up on people.

Jumping Up: Using the leash, pull downward, applying pressure on the dog's muzzle. His entire body will return to the ground. As soon as all four feet touch the floor,

Head-halter correction for jumping up.

Head-halter correction for excessive barking.

Having the dog sit serves as an immediate solution for many problem behaviors.

praise him and tell him to sit. When he sits (whether you have had to place him in position or not), pet him in a favorite spot.

Mouthing: Pull forward and up on the leash. This will close the dog's mouth and pressure him into a sitting position, which is less dominant than standing, yet not as submissive as the down.

Barking: Pull forward and up, staring the dog in the eyes as you say "No Bark" in a low tone of voice.

Aggressive Lunging: Make the dog perform a sit. If he pulls toward another dog or person, pull forward and upward and tell him to sit. When he attains this position, praise him but be ready to apply the correction as often as necessary to cure the problem. It also helps to remain calm and

Head-halter correction for growling.

maintain a loose leash. The most common reaction is for you to tighten the leash and scold the dog. This is exactly the opposite of what you should do. This creates a worse problem by conveying your own insecurities to the dog, making him believe that he needs to take over and be in charge. Instead, work him through the situation by returning to your training as soon as possible.

Growling/Snapping: Pull forward and upward, staring Lucky in the eyes as you say "No!" in a low, growly tone of voice. Continue to hold him in this manner until he blinks and stops growling. Then, return to work in a relaxed manner. Never show that you've been frightened. This causes a wavering in your voice and hesitation or shaking in your actions. Dogs pick up on these signals immediately and take advantage of your weaknesses.

Head-halter correction for lunging at a person or another dog.

FUN AND GAMES

Around the world, mixed-breed dogs are becoming recognized as helpful partners for the physically challenged, as stars of television shows and feature films, as competitors in performance events and showing the world that they are talented, beautiful and wonderful companions just like pure-bred dogs. Rescue organizations are popping up all over, with an emphasis on "no-kill" shelters, foster homes and rehabilitation for those fabulous dogs who have been misunderstood, abused and neglected and now have a second chance. With Internet access, you can locate dogs all over the country that are adoptable through rescue organizations or who can be adopted directly from a shelter, where they may be in danger of euthanasia. Not all shelters are "no-kill." Rescue groups try to save and rehome as many dogs as possible from the numerous "kill" shelters, but they can't save them all. A popular website is Petfinder, www.petfinder.org, which allows you to search for shelters, rescue groups and even specific types of pets in your area. Also ask at the vet's, groomer's and pet-supply shops about local rescue groups. Groups often hold adoption events at some of these locations.

ACTIVITIES WITH YOUR MIXED BREED

Mixed-breed dogs now have their own clubs, like the Mixed Breed Dog Clubs of America (MBDCA), which offers obedience, tracking, retriever tests, lure coursing and even conformation showing for mixes. Likewise, mixes have acceptance from several pure-bred dog clubs, like the United Kennel Club (UKC), which welcomes spayed and neutered

The basic levels of obedience competition test a dog's knowledge of basic commands like the sit/stay. In more advanced levels, the dog performs the exercises off lead.

mixed breeds into their obedience, agility and weight-pulling competitions. Mixes compete and earn titles right along with the purebreds in UKC events. To compete in the UKC, mixed-breed dogs must be at least six months old and have a UKC Limited Privilege (LP) number. Owners should apply for these numbers well in advance, as participating dogs must have their numbers on the day of the event, not pending. Let's take a closer look at UKC events and some other clubs that welcome mixed breeds.

OBEDIENCE TRIALS

There are three levels in UKC obedience competition, each progressing in difficulty. The first is the Novice level, in which the dog is required to honor, heel on leash and in a figure-8, heel off leash, stand for examination, return to his handler over a jump and perform a long sit. The Open level includes a few of the Novice exercise but adds a drop on recall, retrieve and broad jump. The Utility level is the most difficult of the three; exercises include heeling, scent discrimination with metal objects and various directed exercises, meaning that the dog is away from the handler and follows directions to retrieve, come and jump.

It is interesting to note the "honor" exercise at the Novice and Open level, which distinguishes UKC obedience from that of other organizations. What this means is that for a portion of the exercises, there are two dogs in the ring at once. While one dog performs the given exercises, the "honoring" dog must stay in the ring in a down position, allowing the other dog to work undistracted. This is an important aspect of UKC competition, as it emphasizes a dog's ability not just to follow his handler's direction but also how he behaves as an overall canine citizen.

Each exercise at each level is assigned a given number of points, with the maximum available points at any level 200. To earn a qualifying score, a dog must meet two

Practicing on-lead heeling, a basic obedience exercise.

Make any kind of training "rewarding" for your dog. A treat now and then will keep him motivated and enjoying his practice session.

scoring criteria: his total score must be 170 or higher, and he must have earned more than 50% of the points available for each exercise. For example, the Novice-level long sit is worth 30 points, so the dog must earn more than 15 points for that exercise. He must meet the same criterion for each exercise in the level, with the combined points earned for all exercises totaling at least 170. The judges' considerations in scoring include precision in completing the exercises, teamwork between handler and dog, overall behavior of dog and attitude of handler. Of course, owners must have their dogs under control at all times and dogs must demonstrate sound temperaments. A judge has

the right to excuse any dog whose temperament is questionable or who does not behave politely in the ring.

The titles awarded are as follows: Novice level, United Companion Dog (UCD); Open level, United Companion Dog Excellent (UCDX); and Utility level, United Utility Dog (UUD). A title is awarded to a dog who earns qualifying scores at three different UKC competitions and under at least two different judges. The titles are awarded progressively, meaning that a dog must first earn the UCD to earn the UDCX and so on. To earn the lofty title of United Obedience Champion Dog (UOCH), a UUD must continue to rack up wins and accumulate obedience points. The United Grand Obedience Champion (GOCH) is the highest title awarded in UKC obedience and truly recognizes the cream of the UKC obedience crop.

The MBDCA offers obedience competition and similar titles to that of AKC but with the prefix MB (standing for mixed breed) in front: MB-CD (Mixed Breed Companion Dog), MB-CDX and so on. The American Mixed Breed Obedience Registry (AMBOR) maintains a registry of mixed-breed obedience competitors and a ranking system according to UKC obedience statistics. This organization maintains a similar ranking system for mixed-breed agility and sponsors its own agility competitions as well.

OTHER PERFORMANCE EVENTS

Other competitive events include tracking, agility and flyball. Before deciding on which to pursue, you must take into consideration the breeds (and thus the instincts) in your dog's lineage. Specific breeds tend to perform better on tasks meant for their special characteristics. Sporting breeds work best in field trials and hunting tests; herding dogs excel naturally at herding trials; scenthounds outsniff the rest in tracking. Challenging a variety of skills and coordination, agility and flyball offer a more varied structure, with more of an opportunity for any breed to compete. However, in these events, the competitor must be very well trained, agile and quick, making herding breeds the most successful exhibitors (especially Border Collies, German Shepherds and Australian Shepherds). You are at an advantage for this type of competition if one of those breeds is in your mixed-breed's ancestry. However, any breed or mix is capable of success in tracking, agility and flyball, so you might want to give these events a try.

Tracking is very popular with owners of sporting dogs and mixes of these breeds. There are several different levels of competition. The Tracking Dog (TD) title, Tracking Dog Excellent (TDX) title, Variable Surface Tracking (VST) title, and Champion Tracker (CT) title are available to mixed-breed dogs in MBCOA tracking events, which are similar to those of the AKC. Each level requires more and more difficult tracks that include crossing over different types of terrain and even crossing over one's own track. Dogs must find specific articles

This dog flies through the tire jump as his handler runs beside him. Agility is a fast-paced sport for dogs and handlers, and thoroughly enjoyed by spectators.

The agility broad jump requires the dog to attain height and distance.

Amid the fast pace of the agility course, the dog must stop and do a down/stay on a platform.

with the tracklayer's scent on them and sit and/or bark to announce the find. Points are lost for leaving the track at any time, for missing an article or for taking an extremely long time to finish. Many mixed-breed dogs excel at tracking and go on to make very good search-and-rescue aids.

Agility will test your dog's aptitude for overcoming obstacles and figuring out puzzles. This sport really stimulates dogs' minds and exercises their bodies, and the same goes for the handlers! Everybody has a raucous good time, cheering each other's dogs over the obstacles. The obstacles include an A-frame, a see-saw, high jumps with solid panels or poles, a broad jump, pause table, hurdles, a tunnel, a collapsed tunnel and weave poles. The more each competitor accomplishes, the more challenging the course becomes. Dogs are scored on both speed and accuracy in navigating through the course. Mixed breeds can compete in AMBOR-sanctioned agility trials, as well as those sponsored by the USDAA (United States Dog Agility Association) and NADAC (the North American Dog Agility Council), among others.

Flyball promises fun for all. The only prerequisite is to have a dog that enjoys retrieving. The sport is done as a relay race. Two teams of four handlers and dogs take turns having their dogs run to the flyball box, trip the mechanism that shoots out a tennis ball and then fetch the ball. As soon as one dog returns with the ball, the next dog on the team is sent to the box. In advanced flyball, the dogs have to go over hurdles on their way to and from the box.

Here is a listing of Internet sites that offer information on mixed-breed clubs and others that allow mixed breeds to compete: UKC, www.ukcdogs.com; AMBOR, www.amborusa.org; USDAA, www.usdaa.com; NADAC, www.nadac.com; and MBDCA, http://members.tripod.com/mbdca.

TRICKS

If you don't wish to compete with your dog, you can have fun and keep the two of you busy by teaching him tricks. Who knows? Your mixed-breed dog could be discovered and become the next canine star! Tricks can be taught while you and your dog are working on basic training. In fact, taking a break now and then from the routine and teaching a trick can make a training session more exciting. Teaching how to shake a paw is a great place to begin. However, if your dog is one who tends to put his paw on you for either dominance or attention, you must remember to enforce the canine "all or none" law, which means keeping his paws off you until he learns that dominant behavior is not acceptable.

Your well-trained mixed breed must be reliable in a sit/stay before you can begin. Many dogs will become very excited when performing tricks and need to stay calm enough to listen while distracted. Here's

Teaching the dog to "shake"—start by facing the dog while he is in a sit/stay.

Holding the treat, move the dog's face to one side as the other hand taps his foreleg.

The treat is given to the dog as your hand holds his paw.

how to teach Lucky to give you a paw to shake.
1. Place the dog in a sit/stay and face him.
2. Hold the treat in one hand (this will be your target hand) and place your other hand, palm up, near the leg you wish to shake with.

Progressing from the shake to the wave.

3. Using your target hand, bring the dog's head to the side as you say "Lucky, shake." As his head follows the target, his weight will also go in that direction, taking it off the leg you wish to lift and shake.

4. Tap the lifting leg with the fingers of your outstretched hand. When he moves that leg, praise him (click your clicker) and give him the treat.

This exercise, as with all exercises, will use successive approximation. Each time you have the dog do this trick, you will require that he completes more of the criteria toward the final result before he receives his praise and reward. If using a clicker, click at the second that Lucky shows the proper response and give him his treat.

The first time you ask for the shake, all you'll require is for the leg to move. The second time, you'll require the leg to lift slightly. Each successive request for "shake" will require Lucky to lift his leg higher. As he learns to lift his leg, so will he also acquire two targets. The first will be his nose following your hand. The second will be his foot aiming for the upturned palm of your other hand.

At first, target number two is held very close to the ground so that Lucky doesn't have to lift his leg high to accomplish the minor goal. He'll quickly discover that the behavior you are looking for is for his foot to touch your hand. The first time he does so, give him lots of praise and a treat. Each time, hold your proffered hand a little higher. The dog must, therefore, lift his leg higher to achieve the second target.

Most dogs accomplish this trick within a few training sessions. Due to your making it possible to achieve this goal quickly through your use of shifting his body position and building on small successes until reaching the end goal, Lucky will not ever become confused.

Once your dog is doing his "shake" trick for a few weeks, you can start to ask for a right or left shake. All you need to do is begin pairing the words "right" or "left" with your current "shake" command, then switch the signals, gradually building on the criteria for the other side. Be sure to switch your target hands accordingly.

The next behavior you can teach is the "wave." Your gifted mutt already has the building blocks for this exercise, because he already lifts his paw on command. Transferring the shake into a wave will require that you first teach Lucky to shake with your target hand at a distance, instead of within easy reach of his lifted paw.

Begin by sitting a foot or two away when you ask for the shake. Now he'll have to reach his paw forward in order to touch your target hand. Be sure to praise and reward him for each minor incre- ment. When Lucky is reliable with stretching his paw forward, tell him "Lucky, wave" as you offer your target hand, just out of his reach. He may not understand the verbal command at this time, but will identify with the visual signal. He'll see your hand out and know that he is to put his paw in it. When he reaches forward, you'll allow his paw to rest in your open palm, but will move it up and down twice as you praise him: "Good Lucky. Good wave."

Do this a couple times, teach- ing the dog that "wave" means his paw will be moved up and down. The next training session, when you ask him to wave, don't let his paw touch your open palm. Keep your hand just out of reach and move it up and down. He will try to put his paw in your hand and

thus will be moving his paw up and down. As he does so, praise him and give him his treat. He just accomplished the wave trick.

Slowly build on the amount of times he waves by making him move his paw once more for each wave request before you give him his treat. Don't ask for more than three or four up-and-down paw movements, though.

Another trick that can be taught from the base of a sit/stay is to sit up on the haunches. This is commonly called the "beg," but we'll call it "sit-up," for begging is actually a behavior problem and not one to be promoted.

Begin by putting Lucky in a sit/stay with his rear end up against the corner of a wall or kitchen cabinet. This type of back- drop will allow him to lean up and back without risking that he will fall over backward.

To teach the "sit- up," begin by having the dog in a sit/stay in a corner to support his back when he sits up.

The trainer's hand is above the dog's head, showing the sit-up signal.

Close-up of the dog's nose near the target during the sit-up trick.

1. Hold your target hand over your dog's head, the treat between your thumb and middle finger, point your index finger skyward and say "Lucky, up." The target hand must not be more than a few inches over his nose or he'll feel the need to leap upward to reach it. Hold the treat almost within reach, but not close enough for him to take it from you.

2. As Lucky strains to take the treat, he'll put all his weight on his haunches. As soon as he does so, praise him and give him the reward (or click and give the treat).

3. The next time you request him to sit up, don't give him his reward until you see his forelegs leave the ground at least an inch. Each time you practice the "sit-up," make sure you require the dog's front feet to leave the ground just a little more each time before he receives his bridge and reward.

You may need to offer a helping paw. Some dogs, especially young ones, have a difficult time with balance, for their skeletal and muscular systems are not yet fully developed. Some older dogs may feel a bit uneasy about this new position. Allow your unsteady student to rest a paw on your arm or hand as his body rises upward to reach his target. This will make certain that he doesn't fall and hurt himself or stop trying due to frustration.

All trick training must be loads

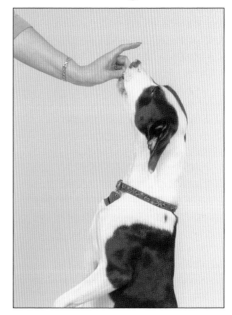

of fun. Should it become frustrating, your dog will lose attention. If this happens, rethink your procedures. Maybe you were asking for too much at one time. Go back to a smaller goal and gradually build on that. All training is a matter of attaining smaller goals before reaching the ultimate goal. Take your time and be very patient. Every dog is different and learns at a different rate. Remember, sometimes you must regress a bit in order to progress.

The next round of tricks can't be taught until Lucky knows how to do a down/stay. These tricks include the tummy-up, roll-over and crawl. They are presented in this order because each builds upon the former.

Tummy-up: This involves teaching Lucky to roll onto his back and remain there until you tell him that the trick is completed. The signal for completion is your praise.

1. Begin with your dog in a down/stay.
2. Show him your target hand, complete with treat inside. Allow him to touch your hand with his nose.
3. Draw his head toward his shoulders as you say "Lucky, tummy-up." When his nose reaches back toward his shoulder, praise and give him his treat.
4. The next time, he doesn't get his reward until his nose actually touches his shoulder. You will

see his entire body start to shift at this point. It has to for him to reach around to properly target on your hand. Be sure to praise (click) him as soon as you see the shift.

5. Keep requesting more and more movement for each successive "tummy-up."

When Lucky reaches the point where he is lying on his back,

TOP: Tummy-up: Start in the down/stay and draw the dog's head to the side with the treat.

BOTTOM: The dog follows the target to the tummy-up position.

The dog stays in the tummy-up.

tummy up, praise him and give him the treat, then tell him to stay, using the same visual and verbal cues used with sit/stay and down/stay. Initially, only make him do so for a few seconds. Gradually, over the course of several weeks, increase the amount of time that he must remain in position. Repeat this trick two to three times, then go back to another trick that Lucky already knows. You should never repeat an exercise more than two or three times in succession. Changing things around keeps Lucky atten-

The dog follows the target into the roll-over trick.

tive and prevents him from developing any type of pattern-training.

Roll over: The next trick builds on the tummy-up. In fact, you are halfway there with the tummy-up trick. The hard part is already done. To teach the roll over, keep the dog's head moving all the way around until he has returned his belly to the ground. Be sure to differentiate the two tricks by clearly telling the dog what you want. The tummy-up has a stay when he reaches the tummy-up position. The roll over has continuous movement from start to finish, without any "stay" command inserted in between. If you distinguish between the two, Lucky will as well.

Crawling: This trick is also done from a down/stay. This must be built on literally one step at a time. Each time the dog makes one move, he must be rewarded.

1. Begin with Lucky in a down/stay.
2. Place his target just out of his reach and say "Lucky, crawl."
3. Lucky will first stretch his neck, then, seeing that he still can't reach his target, he'll reach out with his paw. Praise him (click) and give him his treat.
4. The next time, don't give the reward until he moves two of his feet, and so on, until he's made an entire four-legged effort to reach his target.

You may need to apply light pressure to his shoulder blades to

from him as you request the behavior. Any time he tries to get up, patiently replace him in his down/stay and back up a bit. Remember that you must often regress in order to progress.

With the dog in the down position and the trainer walking forward, the dog follows the target into the crawl.

Now we'll introduce two tricks, spinning around and weaving through your legs, which are easily taught through your targeting methods. Lucky will simply follow his

ensure that he doesn't try to get up and walk to his target. Most dogs will try this. Maintaining the pressure will help Lucky understand that he is to remain in his down position while reaching for his target.

Once you have movement from all four legs, you can increase your criteria to more and more ground coverage with each "crawl" request. Within a few training sessions, Lucky will be able to crawl at least 2 to 3 feet. Gradually, work on increasing your distance

The spin trick: the dog follows the target around and ends up in the sit position before getting the treat.

The weave: the dog walks in a figure-8 around the trainer's legs.

target and gradually associate the commands you use with each exercise. In effect, you are making him successful by offering the same visual cue with each exercise. Through association, Lucky will learn the meaning of the word through the repeated action, just as he learned the meaning of "sit."

Let's begin with spinning around.

1. Place Lucky in a sit/stay and stand in front of him.
2. Show him his target and allow him to follow it in a circle. As you bring his head around, say "Lucky, spin." As he moves his body to follow his target, praise him. This will encourage him to continue. When the circle is complete, give him his treat along with more praise.
3. As Lucky becomes adept with one circle, add another. Within a short time, Lucky will be spinning around and around. He can also begin associating the amount of times you wish him to spin by your saying, "Lucky, spin three," or "Lucky, spin four."

For weaving through your legs, you must also allow Lucky to follow your target hand.

1. Spread your feet apart far enough so that Lucky can slide through your legs.
2. Show Lucky his target from in between your legs. As soon as he gets up to follow the target, praise him.
3. When he makes a complete pass,

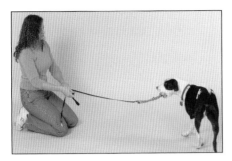

tell him to sit and give him his treat.

Build on the trick by having Lucky follow your target hand around and through your legs before he receives his reward. Next you can do this as you walk. Each time Lucky moves through your legs, give him praise, leaving the treat for completion of the trick. The praise will always encourage him to continue, while the reward tells him when the trick is completed.

RETRIEVING AND OTHER GAMES

If Lucky loves to retrieve, there are many games you and he can play together. The basic ball retrieve only goes so far. A retrieving dog needs a lot of mind stimulation. He can learn to retrieve a specific item, take that item to a specific person (the take-it-to-Harry game) and perform search-and-rescue (the find-it game).

Should Lucky not fully under-stand the idea of retrieving, try the following:

1. Tie a long string to his favorite toy.

2. Throw his favorite toy a short distance away. When Lucky goes for the toy, praise him (click).
3. Once Lucky has his mouth on the toy, begin drawing it closer to you. Praise Lucky as he follows the toy.
4. When you have brought the toy all the way back to you, with Lucky either attached or nearby, praise (click) your dog and give him a reward.
5. Repeat this until Lucky learns the pattern of going after the toy and returning to you with the toy for his reward. When you no longer need to bring the toy back with the string, remove it. Lucky now retrieves.

Never try to teach your puppy

To teach the retrieve, start out by having a toy attached to the end of a long string.

Once the dog has the toy in his mouth, draw the string in close to you, guiding him to bring the toy back.

With practice, the dog will bring the toy back on his own, without the string.

The Small Munsterlander is a breed not too frequently seen in the US, but this mix is a handsome fellow who has taught himself a neat trick!

the retrieve by using force. This takes all the fun out of the game and turns it into something he either must do or be punished for not doing. This is not a positive approach to training. Take your time and make sure that your dog enjoys retrieving. Praise and reward for each little increment of success. Every dog is different. Some may quickly pick up the concept, others may take longer.

Teaching your dog the names of his toys may take a bit of patience and persistence, but it is well worth it. Imagine the fun of asking him to fetch his ball, bone or stuffed toy, and his returning to you with the toy you asked for. Once your happy retriever understands the names of the toys, you can hide several of them and ask him to find a specific one. This teaches Lucky tracking and discrimination skills, both of which can be utilized in competition and real work, such as obedience trials, search-and-rescue, substance detection and hunting.

Begin by discovering which toy Lucky likes the best. Observation and testing will help in this process. Try throwing several toys at the same time. The one he goes to first is his favorite. Begin teaching the name of the toy by repeatedly using the name when you tell him to fetch it.

Try throwing two toys: his favorite toy and another toy, something he rarely shows interest in.

Ask him to bring back his favorite, using the toy's name. Should he return to you with the other toy (however unlikely), send him again. Lucky only receives his big reward—your lavish praise (click) and a treat—when he returns to you with the toy you had asked for. Dogs can discriminate between a little reward and a big one. They will always try to get the biggest reward possible. Thus, in using this method, Lucky will quickly learn the concept.

Once Lucky is regularly retrieving his favorite toy, add a little more difficulty by placing three of his toys a short distance away. Tell him to fetch his favorite, using its name: "bone," "ball," etc. Most likely, he'll return with the one you requested no matter how many toys you put in the same location because it's his favorite and he's learning its name.

The next step is to put away the favorite toy and use his second-favorite. Use the same procedures as with the favorite toy. Lucky will be learning the name of his second-favorite toy as you proceed to work on this trick. Once he knows the toy's name, it's time to make him really think.

Let's say his favorite toy is a ball and his least favorite is a rubber bone. Place both toys together a short distance away. Ask him first to fetch his ball. When he returns with it, praise him and offer him a reward, such as a treat.

You can use your dog's retrieving skills for practical purposes. This owner never loses her keys!

Next, ask him to retrieve the other toy. Always praise him when he returns with the toy.

Now place both toys together a short distance away and then ask Lucky to fetch his bone first. Should he bring back his ball, ignore him and send him again, asking for the toy you want by name (in this case, "bone"). At first, he'll be a little confused. After all, he did bring back his favorite toy. Continue to ignore him until he starts to go for the right toy. As soon as he does praise (click) him. When he returns with the bone, praise him lavishly and offer him a treat. Continue to mix up which toy you send him for. This teaches Lucky to listen for the name of the toy before retrieving it.

This game can be expanded, one toy at a time. As Lucky learns the names of each toy, there are many different games you can play. Not only does this expand Lucky's mind, it's also a fun challenge for you.

The take-it-to-Harry game will give your entire family hours of fun. Begin by asking Lucky for a specific toy. When he brings it to you, point to someone, say their name and tell him, "Take it to Harry" (you can either insert the person's actual name here or find a new friend or lost relative named Harry). That person should ask Lucky to come and praise the dog as he nears. As soon as he arrives, that person takes the toy, praises (click) and gives him a treat. That person then tells the dog to get another toy and, as soon as he picks it up, that person tells the dog to whom he should deliver it. That person then calls Lucky to come, and so on. Not only are you teaching your dog the different names of his toys, you are also teaching him the names of your family members and friends.

The find-it game can also be great fun. Place Lucky in a sit/stay or down/stay and place one of his toys a short distance away. Go back to Lucky and allow him to see the toy as you send him to fetch it. When he returns with the toy, give him lots of praise and a treat. Repeat this a few times, placing the toy farther and farther away. As Lucky becomes adept at fetching the toy that you name, begin to hide it halfway behind something and then tell him to fetch it. Lucky should still be able to see a part of it.

The next step is to completely hide the toy. Tell Lucky to find it. He'll put his nose to the ground and search. As soon as he locates the toy, praise him. When he returns to you with it, give him more praise and a treat.

With Lucky able to distinguish his toys by their names, you can enhance the game by hiding several of his toys. Ask him to find a specific one. When he returns with that toy, give him his reward, then ask him to find the next. Wouldn't it be great if Lucky could find your keys or glasses when you lose them? These items can be added to his repertoire as easily as any toy, though be careful he doesn't start to consider your glasses as a toy! Lucky will enjoy finding whatever object you request him to retrieve. Not only will this stimulate his mind, it will also prepare him to be a good service dog, should that be one of your future goals.

THOSE MARVELOUS MIXES!

A mixed-breed dog is as valuable and lovable as any pure-bred dog and can perform in the same capacity or even better than some purebreds, for they retain the characteristics and behavior patterns of their diverse lineage. Don't let the fact that your dog is of mixed heritage keep you from developing his full potential as a happy and loving

A mixed-breed dog can be a girl's best friend!

individual. Lucky is one of a kind. There is not and never will be another just like him. Offer him a fulfilling life through positive interaction and stimulation and he'll show you loyalty and love unlike any other being on earth.

This young woman and her mixed-breed companion are looking forward to many years of the special friendship forged between owner and dog.

INDEX

*Page numbers in **boldface** indicate illustrations.*